T0356150

Praise for *Unleash Your Financial Superpowers*

"Greg Luken's *Unleash Your Financial Superpowers* is a refreshing approach to personal finance, giving readers simple, actionable tools to build financial security. With clear guidance on wealth building, this book empowers you to make confident, informed decisions and reach your financial goals."

    — **BRANDAN WRIGHT**, former NBA player

"If you grew up in a family without a lot of money like I did, you'll appreciate this book for honoring the challenges and struggles that upbringing comes with. Luken communicates directly in clear, simple language that is great—even for artists like me who don't speak financial-ese!"

    — **KYE FLEMING**, Nashville Songwriters Hall of Fame
      inductee

"Another great book by Greg Luken. I wish I could have read this fifteen years ago. Greg has an incredible ability of making the topic of money approachable and fun."

    — **BRADFORD VIEIRA**, regional president and CEO of
      ServisFirst Bank

"Greg Luken's *Unleash Your Financial Superpowers* is a powerful guide to financial mastery. With real-life examples and practical strategies, Greg shows how the first-generation wealthy overcame challenges to build lasting success. His insights on purpose, planning, and execution provide a clear path for all people who are ready to take control of their financial futures. His passion for this work shines through in every chapter."

    — **GINGER JONES**, serial entrepreneur, consultant, and speaker

"*Unleash Your Financial Superpowers* is a fun take on a serious subject. Greg Luken merges his astute financial knowledge with personal stories and pop-culture references to create a memorable, accessible, and useful guide to financial success. I think everyone can learn something here, and if you are only going to read one book on financial planning, this is it."

— **NELSON ANDREWS**, president of Andrews
Transportation Group

"Unleash Your Financial Superpowers isn't just a book, it's an actionable, step-by-step guide on how to build and maintain the wealth your family deserves. It's obvious Luken has been doing this for decades because every exercise and story is rich with wisdom and clarity. Every family should read this book together; it's the best bonding experience that will provide dividends for decades."

— **AMANDA HOLMES**, coauthor of the best-selling book
Ultimate Sales Machine

"*Unleash Your Financial Superpowers* confronts the reality faced by so many working moms like me who are leading a company or have a demanding career. We are raising kids while also caring for our aging families, and it seems that our own financial concerns come last. This book meets entrepreneurs and professionals where we are. It lets us know we're not alone, and lays out a clear, straight-forward path for making intelligent decisions in an increasingly complex world."

— **DEEANNAH SEYMOUR**, CEO and cofounder of pH-D
Feminine Health

"Like many Americans of my generation, my parents divorced, we lost our house, and endured some lean times. Moving from that world to one with money managers, tax accountants, and attorneys is a major shift. *Unleash Your Financial Superpowers* gives voice to the journey, provides practical advice for facing the challenges, and, more importantly, lays out how to unleash the superpowers we all possess."

    — ROBERT CAREY, CFA and chief investment strategist at First Trust Portfolios L.P.

"Many first-generation wealthy discover the lessons Greg Luken lays out in *Unleash Your Financial Superpowers* too late. Packed with practical strategies and eye-opening insights, this book equips you with the knowledge to sustain and grow your wealth. From navigating financial pitfalls to cultivating the right mindset around your money, this is an essential guide for anyone seeking to keep and grow wealth for not only a successful future but a satisfying life as well."

    —TRACI SCHUBERT BARRETT, author of *What If There's More?* and founder of Navigate the Journey

"*Unleash your Financial Superpowers* is a must read for any entrepreneur looking to tap into the secret ingredients for creating and sustaining success. Greg Luken has successfully identified the *it* factor that influences whether your life is one of triumph or tragedy."

    — SHAY ESKEW, 51x IRONMAN finisher, and best-selling author of *What the Fire Ignited*

"*Unleash Your Financial Superpowers* is an engaging guide that demystifies financial principles even for nonfinancial people. Luken tackles obstacles that often hold people back and equips them to make solid decisions in an increasingly confusing world. His approach is both lighthearted and supportive, making complex topics accessible and enjoyable without any sense of judgement."

— **JAY HOOVER**, CPA, CFP, managing member at Baker Sullivan Hoover PLC

UNLEASH YOUR FINANCIAL

SUPERPOWER$

HOW THE FIRST-GENERATION WEALTHY DO IT
AND HOW YOU CAN TOO!

GREG LUKEN

Forefront
BOOKS

Published by Forefront Books, Nashville, Tennessee.

Distributed by Simon & Schuster.

Library of Congress Control Number: 2024921257

Print ISBN: 978-1-63763-372-4
E-book ISBN: 978-1-63763-373-1

Cover Design by Bruce Gore, Gore Studio, Inc.
Interior Design by Bill Kersey, KerseyGraphics

Printed in the United States of America

Dedicated to

Sheryl Crawford Luken (1941-2024).

Thank you for showing me

what unconditional love is.

TABLE OF CONTENTS

IS THIS BOOK FOR YOU?

IF YOU'RE TRYING TO FIGURE OUT A SIDE HUSTLE TO pay off your credit cards, that's great ... but this book isn't for you.

However, if you've already built some wealth and experienced some financial success—maybe you're out of debt and are actively investing and halfway to your first million dollars; maybe you've crossed the million-dollar net worth figure for the first time; or maybe you've become a first-time decamillionaire—then there's probably something here for you.

This book presupposes you've already built a wealth engine through consistent, systematic investing; building equity through your company by direct ownership or stock options; selling your own company; or all the above.

This book also presupposes that you have untapped potential and you'd be willing to unleash it to help the people you care about. If this sounds like you, then let's get started!

CHAPTER 1

RELATING TO MONEY

EVERYONE HAS A RELATIONSHIP WITH MONEY. AND like most relationships, it can be complicated.

Not *yours*, of course. You're logical.

And if you're married, it's probably not you who's having trouble—it's your spouse who needs to get a grip on their relationship with money.

It's always the other people.

Not you or me.

We're fine.

Really.

For more than three decades, I've had the opportunity and privilege of working with, helping, and learning from financially successful families. I've seen what I call "Financial Superpowers" at work firsthand; I've witnessed the Seven Deadly Financial Villains who are hell-bent to get you off track; and I've discovered practical strategies to overcome those scallywags and close the gap between where you are today and your potential to create, protect, and enjoy wealth—the way you want to. Leo, my dad (aka "Pop"), taught me I could learn something from everyone I meet. That includes learning what to do—and what not to do. He taught me to watch what others did and notice the results they got—to look for the patterns. And so I did.

Anywhere superpowers and villains exist, there must be superheroes to wield those powers and vanquish those villains. And that's where you come in. All superheroes start off as ordinary beings. Until something beyond their control happens to them. It may be a spider bite, a disintegrating planet, or a family tragedy. But whatever that outside force is, it doesn't end there. The event is followed by a period of learning and maturing and refining as the incident and newfound powers are acknowledged and their full potential is achieved.

You have the potential to be that financial super-hero of your own story. We're going to walk through how others have unleashed their financial super-powers, and I hope it inspires you to unleash yours.

We're all a little quirky with money. (I hesitate to use the word *weird* because it seems a little harsh, although probably accurate.) There's a logical reason we're quirky: it's our stories. We all have stories about money. We've seen how our parents behaved with money. We've watched our friends make decisions with money. We've known people with an astonishingly vast supply of it, and we've seen others with none of it. Too often, the subject is treated like sex or religion: Polite people don't talk about it, and if you do, you risk being crude, rude, or socially unacceptable. You risk becoming an outcast when your ideas or attitudes don't align with the tribe.

We've heard all the warnings: Money is the root of all evil. The *love of* money is the root of all kinds of evil. More money, more problems. A fool and his money are soon parted. Only bad people have money. Most rich people are dishonest. Money doesn't buy happiness. (Pop would often tell me money doesn't buy happiness... but neither does poverty.)

I'll say it again: We *all* have a relationship with money. And, despite our protests, we all have a *complicated* relationship with money. Even you. Even me.

While those relationships are all unique, just as every human being is unique, there are some underlying commonalities and patterns that emerge.

Too many of the most financially successful "first-gen wealth" families are drifting financially, moving toward a vague, shifting, ephemeral dream of *financial somethingness* that *might* happen *someday*. But they're not sure it can or will happen. It may just all go away.

Enter overwork, stress, and anxiety.

The opportunity right now, today, is to change your framework, structure, and outlook toward money so you can reduce stress, enjoy success, have a richer life, and be more available to the people around you. That is what working with successful families with first-generation wealth has taught me. I want you to experience that too.

For most of my life, I felt like there was this huge gap between what I had accomplished and my potential. Maybe most people feel that way.

We all have vast potential, but most of us have not tapped into what we are truly capable of. You have the potential to develop your own financial superpowers. You can start where you are and make smart decisions to maximize what you have in order to end up with a life you truly want.

In the pages ahead, I'll show you how to make choices in order to gain freedom and the ability to do what you want to do. I'll cover a simple game plan that can lead to mastery over your finances—enabling you to control your money instead of letting your money control you, as so many people do. (You *are* the boss of your money, you know.) And I'll take you through a simple process for connecting your money to your unique purpose.

Here's what I hope you'll get out of this book:

- Discover the three key financial superpowers.

- Expose the Seven Deadly Financial Villains who are intent on getting you off track.
- Discover strategies for defeating the Seven Deadly Financial Villains.
- Identify common money mistakes and how to avoid them.
- Get a vision of what's possible for you.
- Learn simple ways to create a plan, get on track, and make it happen.

My hope is that the ideas and principles I'll share, along with stories from my own and my clients' personal experiences, will inspire you to unleash *your* financial superpowers. These stories (with the names and/or details changed to protect identities) are set apart so the ideas and concepts are communicated in story form.

But first, I suppose we need to address the elephant in the room. . .

WHY LISTEN TO ME?

Who am I to tell you what to do with money? I'm not a billionaire, a celebrity, or an internet influencer, nor do I play one on TikTok. However, I may be the most fortunate person on the planet. Every success, failure, setback, and dead end in my life has worked together to get me exactly where I am today.

It may *look* like I planned it out in detail thirty-five years ago, but I didn't. I've just done what Pop taught me: I've watched what other people were doing and paid attention to the results they got. Then I tried to emulate the good … and avoid the bad.

I've been fortunate to work with people who were successful—not just financially but also in the way they have chosen to live their lives. Many of them would probably not use the words *purposeful* or *intentional* to describe how they have lived, but that's exactly what they've done.

I have worked with first-gen wealth. They made it. They earned it. They came from humble or modest beginnings, and, through hard work and by continually developing their skills, they built wealth that seemed beyond their reach in their early years.

I've had the privilege to work with clients who have earned Grammy Awards, performed surgery on thousands of people, started businesses, clothed America's military, administered healthcare on the battlefield, collectively written more than fifty books, and helped countless people in various aspects of their lives. They've hiked Kilimanjaro, gone diving in the Galapagos, discovered ruins in South America, and built healthcare clinics in Congo. These are people committed to making a difference; they are working with a sense of purpose, intent on doing quality work and providing quality care to their clients, customers, and patients.

And so, my qualifications are that I've had the privilege of working with successful people, learning from them, and recognizing the patterns and precursors to their enduring financial success. I've also gotten to see the patterns of those who consistently destroyed whatever wealth they managed to grow. I've had a front-row seat to both the successful and the unsuccessful, watching carefully what they were doing and what they were getting in return.

It's been a fascinating ride.

FIONA'S FOCUS
(In her own words)

I don't know how old I was. How old are you when you can still stand up in the front seat between your parents? My parents had to drive back and forth from Arkansas to California because my dad was in the navy. I don't remember exactly what they were talking about, but I said, "I guess that means we don't have enough money to buy an ice cream cone?"

They bought me one to let me know things were okay. But we never had a lot of money. That taught me to always be frugal.

Because Dad was in the navy, we moved around and lived in some really cool places. When we lived in Honolulu, we never had money to go out or go to the movies, so our entertainment every night was to drive to the beach where I'd play while the sun set. What more could anyone need?

I was a "folkie," and there weren't a whole lot of girls writing songs, playing guitar, and singing in those days. I started playing clubs when I was sixteen doing my own songs. Bars liked it because I was cheaper than a band and, being a girl, it was unusual. It was just "pass the hat" at a lot of places, but I always made good money. Performing my music is basically the only job I've ever had.

I don't know exactly why I booked myself in a hotel bar in Tulsa for a week or two—it was the only time I ever played in Tulsa. One night, a table of five guys was down front. On break, one of them called me over. It was Elvis's band, and the guy that called me over was Jerry Scheff (the bass player). I mean, what are the chances Elvis's band would be at that place on that night during that one time I was in Tulsa?

Jerry connected me with a publisher in LA. I drove out there, signed right away, and had my first song on a record. I was nineteen.

My parents always believed in me. They believed in me more than in their own advice for me. And my belief in myself was strong. I listened to feedback and that reinforced my belief.

I heard about the New York Coffee House Circuit but was told I'd have to come to New York to audition. So, I was off to New York, where I auditioned at the Bitter End and lived very frugally in Hell's Kitchen. Eventually, I moved to Nashville. That's when I wrote my first number one song.

I've always been frugal. But I don't understand money and I never cared to learn about it. I just wanted to do my music. I've been fortunate to have really great people around me who take care of all the money stuff—people who have my back. People who put together a plan for me and made sure it happened. That way I've always been able to do what I wanted.

I've always been content and focused. I enjoyed what I was doing. I knew that what I was doing now— right then—was creating what would come next.

Content and focused. Doubt is the enemy.

Fiona is an inductee in the Nashville Songwriter's Hall of Fame, has written numerous hit songs, and has been BMI Songwriter of the Year (three years), recipient of more than forty-two BMI awards, and the nominee for multiple CMA, ACM, Dove, and Grammy Award nominations. She is an honoree of the Country Music Hall of Fame and Museum's Poets and Prophets series, which honors songwriters deemed to have made a significant contribution to country music.

What I've Discovered

It's difficult to see life's patterns when you're in the middle of living it. It's a lot easier to see how things fit together later, after the story is complete. Looking back on it now, I can see that my whole life has been about learning to recognize patterns.

My first piano teacher, Mrs. Lange, used an interval approach. If you knew the first note, say middle C, all you had to know was the distance, or interval, each note was from the previous one. That way, if you understood the relationship between the notes—the pattern—you could take the song and transpose it into any key.

In high school, I picked up the guitar. Seeing the patterns laid out on the fretboard instead of a keyboard helped me connect the music theory dots. Blues, rock, country, and pop music use some common language, like chord progressions and scales. It became easy to hear patterns of chords and simply pick up an instrument and play it.

When I dropped out of college in Kentucky, I spent two years playing music full-time on the road—performing six nights a week and more than 1,100 sets per year. Later, when I went back to earn my English degree at Baylor University, I learned to recognize patterns in language, seeing the "rhythm" in plot, characters, and theme.

Working in financial markets, I began to recognize patterns that play over and over in that area as well. I began writing computer code in the early 1990s to help distill what those patterns meant.

The common thread running through all the phases of my life was pattern recognition.

By paying attention to the principles and patterns with successful outcomes—as well as the principles and patterns with *unsuccessful* outcomes—I was able to start a firm where our team built a framework to help clients get more of what they want.

Like Pop said, you can learn something from everyone.

You're Different

You're different. You know it. First-gen wealth is different.

You're different from the kids you went to school with. Different from your siblings or parents. And this difference means they often don't understand.

You know what it's like to be middle-class or lower-middle-class. You've been there. You don't want to go back. You've gotten to what feels like a pinnacle . . . and it's lonely. There aren't a lot of people you can talk to about your situation. Perhaps you wonder how to make decisions now that you are in a different bracket. You probably have friends or relatives who are trying to get their credit card debt or spending under control, but that's not where you are anymore. You've gradu-ated from the "tear up your credit cards" advice, and yet you've still got the baggage from your past.

SHEILA KICKS BUTT

Sheila's earliest memory of money is of asking her dad, more than once, to buy a Barbie doll at the store. The answer was always, "No, we don't have the money for that."

Having two deaf parents meant that Sheila had to become more self-sufficient at a young age.

After she got her master's degree and worked for several years as a healthcare professional, she decided to start a business. She said, "My husband, David, would've given me whatever I wanted. He was making most of the money, we have a great relationship, and money has never been an issue for us. But I just couldn't bear the idea of asking him for money to start my business."

She explained, "I needed $500 to get started, to get business cards, do a website, that kind of stuff. I think it goes back to my dad. The reality is, I don't ever want to have to ask a man for money. The only thing I could think to do was to go online and sell some of my jewelry. That's what I did. That's how I got the first $500 to start my company.

"David would've given me the money without even asking me what it was for. But I just couldn't ask. I knew I needed to kick some a** so I would never have to be in the position of needing to ask."

When her company was up and running, David sold his company and stayed home with their young boys for the next decade.

By the time she was in her forties, Sheila had sold her company for a mid-seven-figure payday. Despite being financially successful, generally viewed as formidable among young women, and being happily married, she admits privately that she still has trouble talking to her husband about money.

These psychological obstacles can lead to challenges for the first-generation wealthy, including difficulty in managing wealth effectively, struggles with mental health, and strained relationships with family and friends.

The good news is that there is a framework to free you from these obstacles and unleash your superpowers so you can experience three basic things from your money: autonomy, mastery, and purpose.

Others just like you have used the ideas I'll share in this book—and they've worked.

Your unique relationship with money spans two worlds. There's the world you came from—the world that gave you the motivation, diligence, and persistence to be successful—and there's the world you're living in now where the rules are different.

Psychologically, there may be several things going on with you. You might be dealing with common first-generation wealth struggles, such as

- **Waffle House Hash Brown Life:** Perhaps you feel scattered, smothered, and covered. You've got a ton of responsibility with work and family (maybe caring for your parents along with your kids), and the money stuff has gotten more complicated. You may have accounts or businesses scattered all over the place that you barely have time to keep up with.
- **Imposter Syndrome:** You may struggle with feelings of inadequacy, self-doubt, and believing you don't deserve success or that you will be "found out" as a fraud. This can lead to a fear of failure.
- **Guilt:** You may experience feelings of guilt or shame for achieving success or accumulating wealth while those around you are still struggling. You might feel a sense of obligation to give back or that you don't deserve wealth.

- **Fear of Messing Up:** By far, the most common statement I hear is some version of, "I don't want to make a mistake and mess this up." When the entrepreneur sells the company she's worked her whole career to build, or when the professional decides to cut back or hang it up—and has to rely on his portfolio instead of his skill in the office or operating room—that's when this fear emerges.
- **Control Enthusiast:** You may struggle to outsource or trust others for help. Even though some wealthy people have others do their landscaping, clean their house, change their oil, or help them make smart money decisions, you believe that if you *can* do it yourself, you *should* do it yourself. Plus, if you want something done right, you have to do it yourself. The problem with this is that there's not enough of you to go around.
- **Pressure to Succeed:** You may feel pressure to continue to succeed and achieve even greater levels of success to maintain your wealth and status. This pressure can lead to a constant drive for perfection and fear of failure.
- **FOMO:** The *fear of missing out* can be powerful. You may feel like you're missing out without knowing what exactly you're missing

out *on*. What do wealthy people do that you're not doing? You didn't grow up rich; you don't have a playbook for what this is "supposed" to look like. FOMO can further instill insecurity or avoidance behavior, causing you to procrastinate on critical issues.

MARY KATHERINE'S HAPPINESS
(In her own words)

I always liked having money more than having things. I liked knowing that I could get something if I wanted it. But there wasn't much that I wanted.

Money was tight growing up. But being poor in a small town in Kansas isn't that big of a deal. Sure, there were people who drove Cadillacs and belonged to the country club, but it was relatively homogeneous.

My family didn't have much money and my brother had a lot of health issues. What stands out is when I would say I wished we had this or that and my mom would respond, "Rich people aren't happy." There was something about the way she said it, almost aggressive. And I guess I thought that if I had money, I wouldn't be able to be happy. Plus, I grew up Catholic; there was something about the vow of poverty. If you were a *really* good girl, you know, you'd choose to become a nun.

Another thing my mom often said is, "Women take care of themselves." My dad didn't make much money, so Mom always thought it was good for a woman to have *her own* money and take care of herself.

My sister and I grew up hearing all this, and it impacted us differently. She never liked to work, and she was grumpy about *having* to work.

Not me. I have always loved my work; it was never about the money for me. I haven't made a ton of money, but I've done fine. I still feel a little weird about it, though. Maybe I'm still trying to get over that limited view of abundance and a weird vow of poverty. Lord knows I've been through more therapy than any normal person would ever do!

Mary Katherine is a professor at Vanderbilt University who has put her saving and investing plan in place and continues to dive into the work she loves.

UNDERSTANDING "WEALTH" AND "WEALTHY"

I've used the term *first-generation wealthy* several times already. Just to clarify, this refers to people who have earned their wealth themselves rather than inheriting it. These are people who have worked hard, taken risks, and made smart financial decisions to build their wealth from scratch. It can be event-driven—through the sale of a business or the exercise of stock options—or it can be systematic, built through disciplined, regular, often automatic contributions. Either way, being self-made is a symbol of individualism, success, and achievement. For brevity, going forward, I'll use the grammatically incorrect term *first-gen wealth* to refer not to wealth or money but to the people who built the wealth.

How much money does it take to be considered "rich" in America? It depends on who you ask. According to a survey conducted by the brokerage firm Charles Schwab, Americans believe an annual income of $2.2 million is required to be considered "wealthy."[1] However, the actual number may be lower than this. Average annual income for the top 1 percent of income earners in the United States is around $819,324.

In terms of net worth, the median net worth of the top 1 percent of income earners is significantly higher than the rest of the population. According to the Federal Reserve's recent Survey of Consumer Finances, the median net worth of the top 1 percent of income earners in the United States is around $11.1 million. This means that half of the one-percenters have a net worth greater than $11.1 million and half have less. This is a stark contrast to the median net worth of the overall population, which is closer to $121,700.[2]

Contrary to the common misconception that the wealthy always remain at the top for a long period of time, studies show that there is a great deal of turnover in this category. Depending on the source, anywhere from 12 percent to as much as 30 percent of the population will spend at least one year in the top one percent of income earners.

Additionally, the rate at which people fall out of the top 1 percent of income earners is quite high. According to multiple sources, about 11 percent of people in the top 1 percent of income earners fall out of this category within one year. A study by the National Bureau of Economic Research found that only about 14 percent of people in the top 1 percent of income earners are still in that position ten years later.[3] According to multiple sources, about 60 percent of the one-percenters are not one-percenters a decade later.

Achieving and maintaining top income status can be transient.

Each year, about 170,000 people reach millionaire status in the US. Those first-time millionaires have an average age of fifty-nine years old, according to Fidelity's research.[4]

Although difficult to pinpoint, estimates point to approximately 125,000 people hitting the $5 million net worth milestone annually, and around 31,250 people reaching the decamillionaire ($10 million) mark each year, according to data from various sources such as the Federal Reserve and Wealth-X.[5] While the exact number of people reaching these net worth milestones varies from year to year, this gives us a general idea of how many people achieve these net worth brackets.

But does the wealth "stick"?

Not as often as people think.

Out of the 125,000 or so people reaching the $5 million milestone each year, many of them will lose the distinction. About 22 percent of them will fail to maintain their net worth above the $5 million mark for a span of just five years.

The new decamillionaires are in the same boat. According to multiple sources, about 30 percent of new decamillionaires will fall below the $10 million net worth figure within ten years.

What does this reveal? It shows that there is a fluidity to wealth creation and retention. This data underscores the reality that achieving a high level of wealth, while certainly an accomplishment, is no guarantee of long-term financial success and stability. It takes more than just making it in the first place. The evidence is clear that wealth can be fleeting, even for high achievers.

We all have a relationship with money and it's important to understand that relationship. Maybe it has helped you to a point and now it's holding you back. Your money relationship can develop into a variety of stress points that may not serve you. You may recognize how temporary or fleeting wealth is for most people, as is shown by the stats. And you're aware that there are people and families that create wealth, keep it, and prosper far beyond money.

What have they figured out? How did they unlock their financial superpowers?

CHAPTER 2

YOUR ORIGIN STORY

A SUPERHERO'S ORIGIN STORY IS OFTEN THE defining moment in their life. They were living an ordinary life until something beyond their control happened to them. The origin story encompasses the inciting event that shapes who they are, their motivations, their moral compass, and ultimately, how they behave as superheroes. Characters like Spider-Man, Thor, Iron Man, Hulk, Superman, Batman, and Flash all have unique origins that shaped their identities as heroes.

The hero's origin story follows a specific pattern. The hero who is not a hero yet is living an ordinary life when he or she is acted on by an outside force, something beyond their control. After this event, life is different than it was before. The hero may not immediately understand the impact of the inciting event and its subsequent consequences. It often takes a while for the hero to mature, explore the implications, and learn the boundaries of the change that has been thrust on them. The hero must learn and come to understand their purpose. Finally, the hero realizes more fully how to channel and direct the change that has been wrought on them and connect it to their deep "why," to their personal North Star, and to the core of their purpose.

This is true of superpowers.

And so it is with financial superpowers.

Every hero starts as ordinary, begins to understand their abilities and attributes, and uses their intrinsic motivations to develop and master their superpowers. In every instance, there was something that happened in the development of their character as they began to understand what had been entrusted to them and what they needed to do to develop, optimize, and maximize those resources and opportunities.

Spider-Man, one of the most relatable super-heroes, gained his abilities after being bitten by a radioactive spider (the outside force acting on his ordinary life). The death of his uncle Ben, who imparted the famous words, "With great power comes great responsibility," serves as the catalyst that motivates Peter Parker to focus his changed life to become Spider-Man. This sense of responsibility becomes a central theme in Spider-Man's character, as he commits himself to protecting the innocent and using his powers for good. This moral compass (his deep "why") guides Spider-Man's behavior as he navigates the challenges of being a hero.

You have an origin story when it comes to money. It's unlikely you've been bitten by a radioactive spider, and you may not be aware of your financial origin story, but it's part of you nonetheless.

As a child, you heard adults talk about money, about people who had or didn't have money, and you read between the lines. Within your family, you experienced what money was for, what you had, and what you didn't have. There were topics that were discussed and topics that weren't. You probably had a takeaway from both.

Let's consider some questions: What was your first memory of money? What is that story? What did your parents say about money? What didn't they say? What did you notice about money before you were ten years old? When did you earn your first money? Why did you have a job? Why did you have *that* job? What did you learn about money? What are some of your early money stories? All these incidents and ideas impact your financial origin story.

LITTLE RED WAGON AND THE BLANK CHECK
(In his own words)
Dad was a Boy Scout leader and brought home Chiclets gum for the troop to sell as a fundraiser.

I was about eight years old. I wasn't a Webelo yet, but Dad said I had to sell at least three boxes of Chiclets. So, the next day, I took off with what I thought were five boxes of Chiclets in my Little Red Wagon.

Those boxes were actually cases.

But I was eight. I didn't know what a case was. They looked like boxes to me. And Dad said I had to sell at least three. So, I took off in my uniform, pulling my wagon.

When Dad came home and realized all the Chiclets were gone, he was furious. I tried to explain to him that I sold the three boxes he said I had to sell—and two more. But he wanted to know where the rest of the Chiclets were. He just couldn't believe I had sold them. Until I started pulling out fistful after fistful of dollar bills.

When he finally realized I hadn't sold three boxes but fives cases, he said, "You are going to work for me!"

I worked for Dad some in the summers. But as I got older, our relationship grew very contentious. When I told him I was going to go to college, he basically cut me off. He wanted me to come work for him after high school, but I wanted to get an education.

The summer after I graduated high school, my sister told me about a man who gave scholarships to kids who were down on their luck. He didn't live far from me, so I went over to his house and knocked on his door. I told him that I'd heard about what he did and wanted to apply. He said he hadn't made his decision for the next year and that I could meet him at his office.

When I got to his office in the L&C Tower in downtown Nashville, he had me sit in a chair across from his massive, fancy desk. My chair was so soft and padded that I sank down until my eyes seemed to only reach the height of the desk.

He asked me what I had decided to do over the summer. I told him I was going to sell books door-to-door for a particular book company to earn money for college. He practically jumped across the desk and shook my hand. "I sold for the same company in '53 and '54! You've got the scholarship! I'll give you a check at the end of the summer."

He took me to dinner and introduced me to political folks he knew, like congressmen and people like that. He told them I was going to work for the same company he had sold for, and he knew I would be successful.

His confidence in me blew me away. After all, I had just met him.

Very soon afterward, I got to work selling dictionaries door-to-door. Each week, I was required to send in what I'd collected except for some money for food. The company would take their cut, and then they'd put my cut into a savings account for tuition.

On Sunday afternoons, I would send all my money to the company except for one dollar. There was a diner where I could get breakfast on Monday morning for ninety-nine cents. I'd pay for breakfast and still have one penny in my pocket. That way I knew I wasn't broke. But I knew that if I wanted to eat lunch that day, I had to sell something before lunch.

By the end of that summer, I'd saved enough money to pay for two years of college tuition.

I went back to see the man in the L&C Tower. We talked and caught up, and then he reached across the desk and handed me a check. It was the scholarship he'd promised me. The check was made out to me—but the amount was left blank. I remember just staring at that blank check.

I don't think I had planned on doing what I did next. It's kind of a blur. I just remember telling him, "Your confidence in me was worth so much more than the scholarship money."

I handed the blank check back to him.

He shook my hand, and we stayed in touch for several years after that.

It meant a lot to me. Having him believe so strongly in me gave me the confidence that I could be successful. Once I had success that summer, I knew I could make it on my own.

Mark leveraged his skills by partnering with someone with complementary skills. Together, they built a company that employed more than a hundred people in an economically poor county. They successfully sold it for eight figures, and the company is still alive and well.

Exercise:

As you begin to consider your origin story, spend some time writing the answers to the following questions:

1. What is your earliest memory about money? Where were you? Who was there? What happened? What was said? How did you feel? Write the story with as much detail as possible. What did you learn?

2. What are three experiences with money you had before you were twenty-one? Include where you were, who you were with, what happened, and how you felt. What did you learn?

3. Write about an experience with money when you were first on your own financially.

4. Write again about what you learned from each of those stories.
5. Do you believe all those lessons are still true today?
6. Will those lessons still be true in twenty years?
7. How do you think those lessons and experiences have affected your financial decisions?
8. How has that outlook helped you?
9. How has that outlook held you back?

Now share these stories and what you learned from them with someone else.

For free resources to connect with your origin story, you can access a worksheet from my company's website at www.luken.pro/book

CHAPTER 3

DISCOVERING YOUR SUPERPOWERS

ALL SUPERHEROES HAVE THREE FOUNDATIONAL building blocks for their superpowers. The first superpower would win "most likely to get skipped by people in a hurry." Many don't see the necessity in taking just ten minutes to develop this financial power, often because they think it has nothing to do with money. They may believe it's too touchy-feely or couldn't possibly impact results.

The bad news for this "I'm too busy" crowd is that this first superpower is the most important one. The second and third can exist for a while without the first one, but when life gets challenging, as it inevitably does, the first power will allow you to get back on track.

The price of skipping it always comes back around—usually with consequences we don't want to face.

So, what is this thoroughly unskippable superpower?

Superpower #1: The Power of Purpose

The foundational element—the key to unlocking every other power—is the Power of Purpose. Superheroes know their *why*, their reason for doing what they do.

A hero's why informs their moral code. It is their North Star, the moral imperative that guides their behavior. It permeates everything about them and infuses their essence. It creates a framework for how they live their life and overcome villains, and it feeds their tenacity to save the people or worlds important to them.

Batman's origin story is steeped in tragedy. After witnessing the murder of his parents as a child, Bruce Wayne vows to rid the world of crime and injustice.

Trauma fuels Wayne's desire to protect others and becomes the driving force behind his transformation into Batman. His sense of justice, fueled by personal trauma, shapes his behavior as he seeks to protect Gotham City from evil.

Batman has clarity about the Power of Purpose.

You can have it too.

Unleashing the Power of Purpose requires absolute clarity around what's important to you, your why, and the role money needs to play in your life to support your purpose. Creating clarity around your purpose will tap into your deep why and uncover a clear, compelling vision of your future, a magnetic force that will direct your compass when things get tough—which they will. Connecting your vision of the future to your why will solidify your North Star's location. It will help guide you through life's twists and turns.

The TV show *The Biggest Loser* hosted people who wanted to lose a lot of weight. Early in each season, an interviewer always asked each contestant *why* they wanted to lose weight. Inevitably, contestants got emotional when talking about their why. Their reasons rarely related to inflating their own ego, showing off, or anything selfish. The deep why had to do with other people. A woman wanted to live to see her son graduate from high school, or a dad wanted to live to walk his daughter down the aisle in twenty years. They created a connection and got clarity about why weight loss mattered.

In the words of management guru Peter Drucker, "The best way to predict the future is to create it." [6] Clarity of purpose will help you spell out a magnetic, compelling vision of your future—clarity about what you want, why you want it, and exactly where you are now.

OSCAR'S COMMITMENT
(In his own words)

I started working when I was six years old, picking grapes for raisins in California. We did it to afford clothes for school in the fall. I realized when I was six, picking those grapes, that if you didn't have money, you couldn't do anything. Almost everything takes money. I remember thinking that summer, *I never want to be in a position where I can't do what I want to do. I do not want to be in the position my dad is in.*

My mom always promoted education. She would tell me that if you get an education, no one can take that away from you. It's yours. She also taught me to always sit in the back of the church where you can see all the doors. I had cousins that were drug dealers and things were rough. You always wanted to see how you could get out.

My dad would occasionally come home and say, "We're moving," and we would pack up right then and leave. What didn't fit in the pickup got left behind. (I attended fifteen schools by age fourteen and went to six different high schools. We moved around Southern California, Colorado, New York, Puerto Rico, and New Mexico.)

At one point we moved to Barstow. You could homestead and get ten acres, so we lived in a tent while we (my family) built a house with our bare hands. My mom was Seventh-day Adventist, and there was a religious boarding school in Barstow. We couldn't afford it, but I went and worked while I was there. I went to school from 8:00 a.m. to noon, worked in the school's dorms and poultry farm in the afternoons, and studied in the evenings. Later, at 10:00 p.m., I'd go to work with an overnight laundry delivery service—we'd pick up laundry from hospitals between Thousand Oaks and Barstow.

Of course, I usually fell asleep in class.

After high school, I attended junior college for a year but dropped out when the money ran out. While I was working at a steel mill, Uncle Sam called me up for the army and a tour of duty in Vietnam. Even then, I knew I had to keep working and studying to end up where I wanted to be.

When I got out of the army, the GI Bill helped me go to nursing school. I worked as a nurse and saved up to go back to school to become a certified registered nurse anesthetist (CRNA). I worked as a CRNA for more than ten years at St. Thomas in Nashville to save up money to go to medical school.

I remember in fifth grade, the principal came to our room and pointed to each student, one by one. He said, "You won't amount to anything. You won't amount to anything. You might go to college." When he got to me, he pointed right at me and said, "You won't amount to anything." Can you believe it? The principal. Fifth grade. But that was a motivation for me—to prove him wrong.

I saw that principal in Southern California years later. He asked me what I was doing. I told him I'm a cardiac anesthesiologist. He couldn't believe it.

After telling me this story, Oscar erupted with laughter for a solid fifteen seconds.

Why Is the Power of Purpose So Effective?

When we ask people to do something, our odds of success improve if we provide a reason. That's a foundational principle of human interaction, and it's true whether we're asking something of other people or ourselves.

Research has shown that for small requests it doesn't even have to be a good reason.[7] Virtually any reason will do, as long as we hear the familiar sequence: "Will you _____ (the request), because _____ (the reason)?" Human habit kicks in, and we have a predisposition to say yes.

In the 1970s, before personal computers and printers, Harvard researchers conducted an experiment by having subjects stand in line to make photocopies. They privately instructed one person to walk up to the first person in line and ask to cut, saying, "Excuse me, I have five pages; may I use the Xerox machine?" Sixty percent of the time, the person in line granted permission for the subject to jump in line.

Researchers then had another person try a slightly different script: "Excuse me, I have five pages; may I use the Xerox machine *because I'm in a rush?*" With that simple change, the permission rate to jump in line changed from 60 percent to 94 percent. Simply by providing a plausible reason, the response rate jumped by 50 percent.

They then set up another scenario in which the reason provided wasn't a "good" one. "Excuse me, I have five pages. May I use the Xerox machine *because I need to make some copies?*" Even when they provided a reason that didn't make sense, the person at the front of the line gave permission 93 percent of the time—nearly the same response rate as when a "good" reason was given.[8]

Obviously, there's a limit for how far and how often someone is willing to accommodate another person if their reasons are nonsensical or repeated. Nonetheless, researchers concluded that we use a simple rule of thumb: If we are asked for a small favor, followed by the word *because*, we are hardwired to say yes. This is a mental shortcut. We use shortcuts effectively to avoid the mental energy of going through the cognitive process of making a full decision every time.

And this works.

It works with your money. When you have to make a money decision, the Power of Purpose gives you the *because*. And those everyday decisions and actions stack up over time to make a real difference. Staying connected to your Power of Purpose can help you stay on track financially when life shows up.

LUKE'S MERCEDES

(In his own words)

It was a sunny Saturday morning, and our family had nothing on the agenda until an 11:00 a.m. birthday party my sons were attending. We were all up early, and I decided to do something different. I took the boys to a Land Rover dealership owned by a friend. He had said if they weren't busy, he'd be glad to take the boys on a test ride. We were the first ones on the lot and Nelson, the owner, loaded the three of us into a Land Rover and headed to the test track. The boys were whooping it up in the back seat as the Land Rover made sharp turns, seeming as if it would tip over. After what felt like a carnival ride of fun and adrenaline, we said thank you and got ready to go. That's when I saw the shiny Mercedes in the trade-in section.

Next thing I knew, I was pulling into my driveway in a new car, the boys in the back. I could see my wife looking out through the big picture windows, shaking her head no. I motioned for her to come and get in the car. Again she shook her head. I put the car in park and walked inside to remind her that the boys had a birthday party to get to. I told her, and I quote, "You're going to love this car."

"I know I will," she said. "But I'm not getting in it. We can take them in our car."

"Why?" I asked, thinking that made no sense. "They just traded for it; it's got low miles, it's in perfect condition, and they gave me a great price on it."

"I'm not getting in that car because when we did our Roadmap, you said we would get a lake house for our family, *and then* you'd get an expensive car. We don't have a lake house yet. We've been saving that money for the down payment. I'm not getting in that car."

I froze.

She was right.

It wasn't fun taking the car back. But it was much easier than I thought it would be. When I handed the keys to the used car manager he said, "What happened? Did your wife hate it?" I told him, "Not really. I'm just not going to do it now."

Three years earlier, Kelley and I had completed a Wealth Roadmap. There was no denying it. I had been distracted by the latest shiny object. Why? Because I'm human. Her simple callback to a time of clarity and rationality was all I needed. She reminded me we had agreed not to get the car yet *because* of what we wanted to do for our family first.

I'm so thankful she remembered the priorities we had agreed on. The Wealth Roadmap helped ensure that we were connected to our Power of Purpose, were playing on the same team, and had agreement on the goal we were working toward.

How do you discover, distill, or clarify your Power of Purpose? There are several ways to approach it. Some will say that to get to your deep why, you should ask your five closest friends why they are your friend, pushing beyond the definition of *friend*. That could be helpful but also time-consuming. Some say it takes a spiritual retreat. That may be fun but takes a lot of effort. Bill Bachrach's book *Values-Based Financial Planning* spells out a process for values clarification. I recommend you check out his book for a detailed dive on this values clarification exercise.

I believe that clarifying your Power of Purpose is simple. After all, you already have the answer. It is *your* answer. It is already inside of you, whether you know it or not. This is not about making something up; it is about writing down what is already there (and getting rid of all the stuff that doesn't really matter and is mucking up the water).

The Wealth Roadmap
I believe the most effective way to address the Power of Purpose is with a Wealth Roadmap. The Wealth Roadmap helps with clarification. It places a few components all in one simple document to distill what seems very complex down to the basic components. Those four components are

1. Purpose—clarifies your why
2. Goals—clarifies your what, who, when
3. Expectations—clarifies your how
4. Current Situation—a summary of where you are now

We'll see how this first component fits in with the Power of Purpose. The next three— components two through four—come into play shortly.

Resources to complete your Wealth Roadmap can be found at: www.luken.pro/book

Five Questions Deep

The advisors in my wealth advisory firm use the "Five Questions Deep" method on almost every issue when working with clients. That is, we believe the way to really understand a situation is to go at least five questions deep. The principle is pre-kindergartenish: Keep asking why until there isn't an answer.

This works with discovering or clarifying a sense of purpose and is very straightforward and doesn't take a long time. We start with the simple question: What's important about money? We listen for key words or phrases, ask what's important about that, and continue until the answer is something that can't be expressed with words.

Here's an example (using my answers so as not to expose anyone else's answers) of what that may sound like:

Q: What's important about money?
A: To pay my bills, keep biscuits on the table, and keep a roof over my head.
Q: What's important about paid bills, biscuits, and keeping a roof over your head?
A: Just knowing that the day-to-day is taken care of.
Q: What's important about knowing the day-to-day is taken care of?
A: Because then I won't have to worry about money. It frees up my mental real estate.
Q: What's important about not worrying and freeing up mental real estate?
A: Because that gives me a sense of freedom.
Q: What's important about that kind of freedom?
A: I can focus on the people and projects that really matter.
Q: What's important about focusing on the people and projects that really matter?
A: So I can be available, in the pocket, in flow.
Q: What's important about being available, in the pocket, in flow?

A: That's my purpose. That's my best self. That's part of my faith in action and that is my purpose.

Q: What's important about that?

A: I don't know the answer. Can't put it into words. There's nothing more important than that.

A conversation like this could then be summarized with:

Bills, biscuits, roof | Day-to-day | Frees up mental real estate | Freedom | Focus on people and projects | Available, pocket, flow | Purpose, best self, faith in action

And with that shorthand, it allows me to reconnect with the conversation, the details, and the feelings and emotions surrounding that conversation. Those words are a code. You may not completely understand my code (and I may not completely understand yours), but the important thing is that you understand yours.

When I first went through this exercise and discovered that my purpose was to be available, in the pocket, and in flow, I was very disappointed. I wanted something that sounded more grandiose. I had gone on a spiritual retreat. I had asked friends. And then, with this simple exercise I clarified my purpose in about six minutes. That was almost two decades ago.

And here's why it's powerful for me. Admittedly, the words *available, pocket,* and *flow* may not seem to hold great meaning for you. But to me, those few words evoke how I feel when I am being my best self, best brother, best dad, best son, best leader, best follower, best friend. It reminds me of doing my best writing, grieving with a friend in their deepest pain, blasting down a powdery ski slope, landing a sixty-foot jump like butter on a motocross track, listening to someone who needs a friend, being able to help someone in a way I hadn't imagined I'd be able to. Put simply: my purpose.

Your words, your code, will likely be very different and yet will hold layers of meaning for you that you may have trouble putting into words as well.

Two things are important to note. First, clarifying your Power of Purpose is most effective when had as a conversation with someone else who is intent and interested in listening. You may be tempted to do it by yourself, and you can try, but it's like trying to tickle yourself.

Second, when it comes to the Power of Purpose or the Wealth Roadmap, write it down. Sure, you already know it. I'm sure the "skip it" crowd won't do this…to their own peril. I'm not a neurobiologist so I can't tell you what happens, but just like thinking about something and actually saying it out loud are different, saying it out loud and writing it down is different. It feels different. It impacts your brain differently. I've heard successful families repeatedly say, "Wow. It feels different having it in writing."

Having your purpose in writing (or better yet, the entire Wealth Roadmap in writing) can be a powerful tool for you. And we'll find out why as we fly into our next superpower.

Superpower #2: The Power of Plan

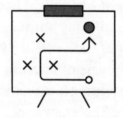

Gaining absolute clarity around your purpose provides the foundation for moving on to the second superpower: constructing a concrete plan of action aligned with who you are.

All superheroes have strength. It may be muscular strength; the ability to fly, become invisible, stretch, or shapeshift; or amazing technology that enables them to create webs, wield an indestructible shield, or fire lasers out of their palms.

Heroes have a plan for dealing with their world based on who they are, their situation, and their strengths. It tells them what to do and when to do it. In the same way, a step-by-step plan of action provides *you* with the strength to get *your* job done.

Your plan should help you reach your goals on time, the way you want, for the reasons that are important to you.

Here is where we go back to the Wealth Roadmap and its four component parts.

In the previous section we covered purpose. Now we'll cover goals, expectations, and current situation.

Goals

The plan should be centered on helping you reach your goals efficiently and on time.

You may have heard that goals should be SMART (specific, measurable, attainable, relevant, time bound). When it comes to financial goals, I think that can make it more complicated than it has to be. I think goals should have four components—always. Financial goals should have

1. Name
2. Date
3. Specific dollar amount
4. Thoughts or feelings associated with their accomplishment

Naming a goal is usually straightforward. It should be something clear and meaningful to you. Some examples of goals I've heard: financial independence, paying for the kids' college, traveling the world, doing what I want. Whatever it is, it should be named.

The date is something that usually takes some consideration and the conversation usually goes something like this:

Q: What date would you like for that goal?
A: I'd like to hang up my spurs and call it a day when I'm about sixty.
Q: What date will that be?
A: In about six or eight years.
Q: And what date should we use, in six or eight years?
A: Let's use six.
Q: So that'll be 2031. And what date in 2031?
A: Let's say June.
Q: And what date in June 2031?
A: Let's say June 17. That's my birthday.
Q: So, June 17, 2031. Does that sound right?

In my experience, this is the conversation virtually every time. This is not a criticism; it is a statement of fact. What that fact tells us is that these financially successful, goal-oriented adults in their forties, fifties, and sixties have often lived decades without clarifying many financial goals. Fast-forward five years, and "six or eight years" can still be six or eight years;

it's mushy. But a specific date is a solid marker. The clock starts ticking.

This level of goal clarification is rarely done. But when it is done, the results are predictably powerful. The date begins to act like a magnet for the goal. Can you imagine having a plan for a goal without knowing when the goal is supposed to be achieved? It's like planning to win a race without knowing when or where the race starts.

Financial goals also need specific dollar amounts. That often means identifying the specific income amount if it were to start today. Something like, "We'd need $30,000 a month for expenses if it were today—and assuming the house is paid off and the kids are out of college and married. We'll want to set up a separate goal for wedding funds."

Finally, there should be thoughts or feelings connected to the accomplishment of the goals. That helps us imagine what it's like to be there, to have already succeeded. Going through the exercise of mentally getting past the finish line of that concrete goal gives our subconscious mind the idea that the goal is a reality, which helps us consciously put the pieces into place to make it happen. Identifying the thoughts or feelings associated with achievement of the goal helps turn it from a wish into a goal. Goals require specific actions and steps to turn them into reality.

We've covered your purpose (your why) and your goals (your what, when, where, and for whom). Now let's cover your how—your expectations.

Expectations

Clearly spelling out your expectations—how you hope to achieve your goals—will provide a reality check and help you evaluate the probability of the outcome you want. Most of us have unexpressed expectations. Expressing those and exposing them to the light of day (or the ears of an advisor, friend, or spouse) helps lay the groundwork for a better experience. Being explicit in our expectations can get us more firmly grounded.

Again, questions are the key. The question to start with: What do you expect?

A conversation could sound like this:

Q: You probably have an idea in your mind of what a successful situation looks like for you— three, five, ten years down the road. Help me understand what that looks like—what do you have the right to expect?

A: Honest communication, responsiveness, advice that moves me forward.

Q: What else?

A: Regular updates, advice that's in my interest. Transparency around costs.

Q: What else?

A: Advice that gets me back on track. Help me gauge the impact of things I want to do along the way. Life doesn't take a straight line always. So when things come up, it helps to have unbiased advice to help make solid decisions.

Q: That's important. What else?

You get the picture. This allows your implicit expectations to become explicit and keeps others— your spouse or advisor—from inaccurately reading your mind. After the list is fully expressed, it also allows any unworkable or unclear expectations to be fleshed out. Reaching alignment and agreement on expectations can help you develop momentum as you move forward.

Armed with purpose, goals, and expectations, you're now ready for the final piece in laying the groundwork: a summary of your current financial situation.

Current Situation

Your current situation is simply a summary or a snap-shot of where you are right now. This should be a balance sheet (which can be distilled down to two numbers: liquid net worth and debt).

With the Roadmap of where you want to go, when and how you want to get there, and a clear sense of your current location, it's time to create a plan of how to get from point A to point B.

Please keep this in mind: I am *not* talking about an eighty-page document (I've actually received one that was 127 pages long) that collects dust in a drawer or on a shelf somewhere. What I am talking about is a living, breathing plan that lays your year out in front of you and shows you what activities need to be done and when they need to be done. Having a clear plan allows you to proceed in a methodical, organized, and thoughtful way to ensure you are leaving no stone unturned.

For example, when I get the oil changed in my car, the technician goes through a thirty-seven-point checklist on the status of my vehicle's filters and fluids. When it comes to your financial life, there should be a much more thorough checklist that either you or your wealth manager is using to direct the process.

So, when it comes to your money, this might mean:

- Planning when and how to review tax consequences and potential tax moves before the end of the year.
- Planning for the unexpected. (The "unexpected" happens with such regularity, you really should expect it.)

- Planning how you will invest during up markets and down markets (and how to tell the difference).

If you work with a financial advisor or wealth advisor already, you may want to ask them for a copy of their checklist. If you don't already work with someone and are considering it, asking for a copy of their checklist is an excellent idea to ensure they have one. You have the right to expect a financial services or financial planning professional to have a more thorough checklist than the oil change guy.

Having a game plan is a tremendous tool that allows you to avoid the mental energy of going through the cognitive process at every step of the way. The plan tells you ahead of time what to do. And with a plan in place, the decision is already made; now, all you have to do is do it.

Part of the Power of Plan is that it eliminates the energy-draining exercise of having to think and make decisions. It's like having a diet—the power of a diet is that it provides a game plan that has some reasonable expectation of positive outcome. Instead of having to decide at every meal whether you are going to eat potatoes, bread, dessert, you just follow the plan.

Having a financial plan also means you should have your own personalized milestones and benchmarks. Celebrating milestones along the way is a great way to create or maintain momentum. This may be celebrating when one of the goals is reached (like Johnny's college fund is fully funded), when a debt is extinguished, or when you hit a milestone dollar amount, like your next million.

A good plan usually leads to the creation of your own index for success as you've defined it. Forget the stock market index; you deserve to have your own index—the "You Index." That way, you can know if you're on track to reach your goals for *your* reasons and to fulfill *your* purpose. Having your "You Index" allows you to have a sense of confidence when you're on the right track and provides you with feedback to know if you're off track and need to make adjustments.

Once you have a robust step-by-step plan of action, you're ready for the next core superpower.

It's the deciding factor.

Superpower #3: The Power of Execution

The third key to unleashing your superpower is the discipline to consistently *execute* your plan.

This is where the rubber meets the road. It's where the real struggle exists because it intersects with decisions we each make every day.

A few years ago, I was on a bicycle ride and had a conversation with fellow cyclist, Peter Vidmar. Peter is a gifted gymnast who qualified for the summer Olympics in 1980 but didn't attend due to the US boycott of the games held in Moscow, Russia. He qualified again in 1984 and was the captain of the 1984 men's gymnastics team at the Olympics in Los Angeles. Peter earned one silver medal and two gold medals in gymnastics and scored a perfect 10 on the pommel horse as he led the team to their dramatic and stunning win against the favored People's Republic of China. He has since been inducted (twice) into the US Olympic Hall of Fame.

As we spoke on the ride, he shared the secret to going to the Olympics and winning medals. I carried away two ideas from our conversation: when to execute and it's the fraction that matters.

When to Execute

One concept we discussed revolves around training and execution. Peter explained that in order to go to the Olympics, one has to train only two times:

1. When you feel like it.
2. When you don't.

Peter understands the discipline to execute.

And you can too.

Execution is simply acting on your plan, connecting it back to your why, and thereby fulfilling your purpose. Since we only need to execute when we feel like it and when we don't, we'll cover ways to make it easier to execute your plan consistently—especially when you don't feel like it. The discipline to execute is something many successful people automate or outsource.

PLAN ON AUTOPILOT
(In his own words)

In January of 2018, I was doing a personal review of 2017. I'd had a lot going on the previous year. I had two kids in high school and everything that goes with that. In the second half of the year, at work we had a key vendor get acquired, which created our most significant operational change in two decades. It was something I never wanted to do again. And I'd sold a business in October. With implementation, due diligence, closing and post-closing work, the second half of the year had been an absolute blur.

Over the Christmas holiday, I was reflecting and pulled out a copy of a Wealth Roadmap that was more than a decade old. I was stunned.

One of my goals—my wife and I had talked about it—was to be in a position where work was optional by November 11, 2017. There it was in writing. Selling the business twelve days before the goal date had made that goal a reality. But I'd been so busy, I hadn't even noticed until almost two months later!

I told my wife. She said, "That's great. I'm proud of you." And then she went back to what she was doing before. She's more of a "role" person than a "goal" person. I called my dad and told him. He said, "Son, you're too young to retire. Nobody in the Good Book retired. You need to keep working at something."

I assured him I had no intention of retiring. It just was going to feel different knowing that I'm not working for a paycheck; I'm working because it's what I want to do.

What was so interesting to me about the whole situation was that for more than a decade we'd focused on that date, we'd invested every month. When we started, we calculated that we needed to invest more each month than we made. It seemed daunting. But we put together a plan, got started, and our plan was adjusted and updated every year. We'd worked to grow the businesses, to make things work; we'd made decisions differently than some of our friends; we'd driven some of the ugliest cars in the neighborhood.

And then it happened—and almost two weeks early! And neither of us noticed at the time.

Would it have happened anyway if we hadn't written it down a decade earlier? I don't know.

But it felt like magic.

It's the Fraction That Matters

Peter and I also discussed another concept we might call "The Fraction Matters."

As Peter explained in his book, *Risk, Originality & Virtuosity: The Keys to a Perfect 10*:

> How often do you hear a parent, coach, or teacher, say, "You better study twice as hard if you're going to get success"? The sentiment makes sense, but the math doesn't. Most of the time, no matter how much we might want to, we simply can't double any significant effort. It's not possible in the case of a world-class athlete. In my sport, any gymnast hoping to make the Olympics must work out at least five hours a day. So if I'm going to double my training, I have to train 10 hours a day. Technically, that may be possible, but from a physical standpoint, it makes no sense. It would be exhausting to the

point of being counterproductive. So, the key to improving isn't to work twice as hard, but just a fraction harder, or smarter, or longer. In the end, it's the fraction that matters. Increase the quality of your effort bit by bit.

It's easy to avoid executing when we don't feel like it because it can seem meaningless. It can feel overwhelming or like what we're doing isn't making a difference. But the fractions, little by little, add up over time. Faithful, diligent execution over time leads to results. Those fractions in results don't show up without consistent execution.

So, we know we need to develop our three key superpowers:

1. Power of Purpose: a clear, compelling, magnetic vision of the future—our why.
2. Power of Plan: a concrete, step-by-step plan of action.
3. Power of Execution: consistent execution of the step-by-step plan.

Those keys will help us deal with the realities of our money galaxy.

CHAPTER 4

YOUR MONEY GALAXY: FIVE REALITIES

WITH SUPERHEROES, WE ARE ASKED TO SUSPEND our disbelief and enter their galaxy. Thor, Aquaman, and Iron Man have different realities that govern the galaxy in which they live. I'm going out on a limb here, but I'm guessing your parents weren't Norse gods or Atlanteans, and that you're not a billionaire playboy who sustained a severe heart injury and invented a suit to escape. And, as a result, you probably don't have the ability to control the wind, breathe unassisted in water, or fly while sustaining massive G-forces.

These three "galaxies" are wonderfully unique, and we view each one through the eyes of our hero. Thor's mythical realm would be foreign to Aquaman's Atlantean perspective, and both of those would seem impossible from Tony Stark's slightly more realistic world of terrorists and weapons of war. Despite their differences, though, each of these galaxies fits in their respective hero's worldview. Each world makes sense to the one living in it.

In the same way, we must explore and understand the world *we* are living in if we truly want to master our financial superpowers and execute our purpose-driven plans. We can call our world our *money galaxy*, and it's made up of five realities:

1. Markets
2. Taxes
3. Time
4. The Four Levers
5. Your Biggest Problem

Let's get to know our galaxy by taking a tour through each reality.

REALITY #1: MARKETS

After several decades of study and having run several hundred million scenarios (my best estimate is slightly more than a billion) using different investment parameters, our firm discovered a few things.

The discovery of this first principle changed my worldview on investing. It has become a significant part of my investment origin story. I call it the Pareto Portfolio Principle®. It makes sense to understand the situation and potential problems to understand efficient solutions.

Who Was Pareto?

Vilfredo Federico Pareto (1848–1923) was an Italian engineer, economist, and philosopher born in Paris into an exiled noble Genoese family. The story goes that while working in his garden, Vilfredo noticed that 20 percent of the pea plants produced about 80 percent of the peas. He had been studying property ownership in Italy and had discovered that 80 percent of the property in Italy was owned by 20 percent of the population. Recognizing this pattern led to his contribution to economics known as the *Pareto distribution*.

The Pareto distribution, popularly known as the 80/20 rule, has been used in many fields. Businesses often experience that 80 percent of profitability comes from 20 percent of customers or that 80 percent of productivity comes from 20 percent of the workforce. In the US, 80 percent of taxes are paid by about 20 percent of taxpayers.

Pareto's 80/20 rule has an application to the way investment markets work as well. But with investments there is an important distinction: 20 percent of the time often yields 100 percent of the results. Simply put, markets tend to spend 80 percent of their time declining and recovering from those declines. Only about 20 percent of the time is spent making money (or, interchangeably, creating capital or hitting new highs). This is a fact most people don't realize.

Let's say you invested in stocks in late 2021. Stocks hit a high in early 2022 and then lost money for most of the year. In 2023, stocks went up. By early 2024, they were back to even. The years 2022 and 2023 were largely spent in decline and climbing back to even. By midyear of 2024 you had some profit, but only after two years of decline and recovery. The reality is, when you invest, you should expect that most days, weeks, and months, you won't be making money. The time spent actually making money, we interchangeably call *new money time*, *capital creation time*, or *new highs*. While this period tends to be the minority of time, it is very powerful.

Pareto Portfolio Principle: Exposing the Truth of How Markets Work

Let's consider this graph of the US equity markets since 1950.

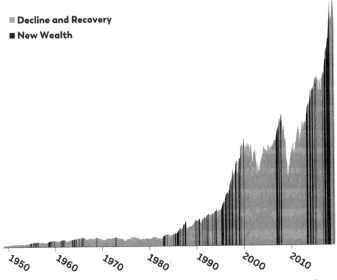

S&P500 Since 1950. Source: Thompson Reuters, Luken Investment Analytics.

Market fluctuations can be categorized into three phases:

1. **Decline:** when markets move from a peak (high) down to a trough (low).
2. **Recovery:** when markets move (recover) from the trough back to the previous peak.
3. **New Money Time:** when markets move above their previous peak to a new high.

Every time markets move from an old high to a new one, new wealth is created. If you invest and the market goes up the next day, you have more money than you did the day before. As I mentioned, we refer to the time the market spends hitting new highs as *capital creation time*, *new money time*, or *new wealth time* because that is when money is made.

In fact, looking back to the turn of the previous century from 1900 to 2018, the research shows that equity markets have

1. Made new money about **15 percent** of the time (the time spent going from an old peak to a new pea).
2. Spent **42 percent** of their time falling (from peak to trough)
3. Spent about **43 percent** of their time recovering from a loss (markets spend more time recovering than falling because they tend to fall faster than they rise)

The Pareto Portfolio Principle is not restricted to US stocks; rather, it affects virtually every type of investment.

SOURCE: YCHARTS, LUKEN INVESTMENT ANALYTICS 12/31/2003 – 12/31/2023.

SOURCE: YCHARTS, LUKEN INVESTMENT ANALYTICS 12/31/2003 – 12/31/2023.

Discovering this principle launched me on a mission. I thought dramatic improvements could be made if a system could reduce a fraction of the time investments spend falling (by moving to less risky investments) so that, with slightly smaller losses, capital creation time could start sooner. Incremental improvements can have dramatic results. If just a fraction of the decline time could be reduced so that capital creation time moves from 20 percent to 21 percent of the time, the result is a 5 percent increase in portfolio efficiency.

I think running a good portfolio should be a lot like running a great business. From that perspective, if a business owner had an employee or vendor who didn't show up to work 80 percent of the time, you can be certain he would do something about it. So I developed algorithms in the early 1990s to recognize patterns that would help improve that new money time ratio. That system became the core of the firm I launched in 1999.

Let me share a little about how it works. Cutting out a portion of the decline (reducing drawdown) causes a portion of the *decline and recovery* phase to shift to *capital creation time*. In other words, removing some of the fall time causes something powerful to happen mathematically: Some of the recovery time is converted to new money time.

A static portfolio is designed to work only in markets that are going up (bull markets). A portfolio designed to work only in bull markets is a portfolio designed to fail you when it counts most. It's important to point out here that there is no system, no silver bullet, no holy grail, no crystal ball that will create 100 percent portfolio efficiency. But as I

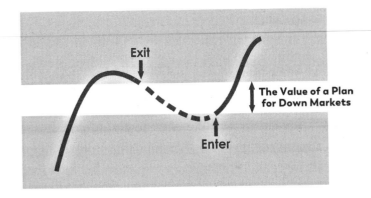

said earlier, incremental improvements can create dramatic results.

A major insight from the Pareto Portfolio Principle is that successful investing requires us to acknowledge the reality that markets spend most of their time going essentially sideways—in decline and recovery phases. This is normal. Even if the Pareto ratio is radically improved, there will still be times when investing can be frustrating. No investment is destined to go up every day, every week, or every year. No investment will go up 100 percent of the time.

Like my Pop often said, "If you didn't have rainy days, you'd only have a desert." So, you can be sure you'll have to wait out more than a few rainy days under even the best conditions—but new money time can make it worth the wait.

Risk Is Dynamic

Another insight we can take away from the Pareto Portfolio Principle is that we need to adjust portfolio *risk* down near peaks (market high points) and adjust *risk* up close to troughs (market low points). Let's unpack this version of "Buy low. Sell high."

Our study of the Pareto Portfolio Principle revealed we can increase the new money time by lowering risk (by investing in more conservative investments) during peaks (high times) in the market and raising risk (by investing more heavily in higher-risk investments) during troughs (low times) in the market.

This finding is significant, because it suggests we should be doing the exact opposite of what we *feel* like doing in each of these phases!

In a sense, being a good investor means running toward danger when our survival instincts are telling us to hunker down. Our brains have evolved in a lot of ways, but becoming naturally good investors is not our evolutionary path.

That is the reality of the galaxy we live in. The fact that we label events with names such as "the Crash of '87" or "the Financial Crisis of '08" is evidence that our brains did not evolve to be naturally good at investing. The root of our investment problem is planted in those headlines. How often do you hear people talk about the "Opportunity of '87" or the "Buying Bonanza of 2008"? Never. And yet, if our brains had evolved to be inherently great at investing, we would likely frame those times as *opportunities* instead of *crises*.

Study upon study and survey upon survey show that investors are generally most optimistic near market highs (like January of 2022 and November 2007), which is when they should be scaling back the risk. Those same surveys reveal that investors are massively pessimistic near market lows (like December 2022 and March 2009), which is when they should be scaling up.

Our brains are wired to lure us into this Dance of Disaster. Like the predictability of a dance, when markets are doing well, we're tempted to adjust our risk up when we should be adjusting it down. When markets have performed poorly and valuations are low, most people despair and get more conservative when they should take a more aggressive stance. It's a pattern like a dance with predictable steps.

Financially successful families understand this. They use a process to help them evaluate risks and make solid decisions in the face of constant uncertainty. Those decisions often fly in the face of the current headlines precisely because they are using tools to look beyond the headlines. A portfolio strategy has to make sense from both a mathematical perspective as well as a behavioral finance perspective. There must be a plan for both up markets and down markets so that people make smart decisions in each.

Identifying Investment Vampires, Zombies, and Phoenixes

Another consequence of the Pareto Portfolio Principle, when it comes to segments or sectors of investments, is that in addition to productive bull market investments, we can identify investment Vampires, Zombies, and Phoenixes.

When a category of investments, such as bonds, US stocks, or real estate, enters a phase where a sustained decline is likely (a down trend or bear market), we refer to those investments as *Vampires*. Why Vampire? Well, when investments (even good-quality ones) enter a time where they're unlikely to be productive, they can *suck the efficiency out of your portfolio.*

One example of this is the Nasdaq 100, an index of one hundred stocks that trade on the Nasdaq exchange. The index (and investments that track it) started going down in the year 2000. It peaked in March of 2000 and was a Vampire until it bottomed out in September of 2002, having lost more than 80 percent of its value. In fact, you could've seen a $100,000 Nasdaq 100 investment in March 2000 turn into $17,004.15 in two and a half years. That's the Vampire phase.

A *Zombie* phase refers to a period when investments go sideways, marked by short-lived periods of decline and recovery. This happens when macroeconomic factors such as regulation, technological changes, interest rates, exchange rates, or other factors affect supply and demand. When this happens to a segment of the economy, most companies within that segment will be affected.

Let's use that same Nasdaq investment we just referenced that started as $100,000 in 2000 with a buy-and-hold approach and lost more than 80 percent of its value in two years. In February of 2009, seven years after that decline, it was worth $22,900. It spent those seven years stumbling up and down like the walking dead.

Fortunately, after going through the Vampire and Zombie phases, an investment might become a *Phoenix*, rising from the ashes of destruction.

The Nasdaq 100 became a Phoenix. After it bottomed out in September of 2002, having lost more than 80 percent of its value, it stumbled along until 2009, with very little return for seven years. Then, from February 2009 through March 2024, it was up more than fifteen-fold. If you bought and held in early 2000, you had to suffer through seventeen years of decline and recovery phases to get back to where you started, which would have happened in January 2017. And then new money time kicked in. By June 2024, that same $100,000 had grown to more than $524,000.

If you'd like to learn more about this topic, you can download resources from our firm's website, www.luken.pro/book.

REALITY #2: TAXES

The winner of the first season of *Survivor*, Richard Hatch, understands that you don't have to pay your taxes, but there are consequences. After winning, he failed to pay income tax on his one-million-dollar prize, the Pontiac he won, rental income, and his income from a radio show. As a result, he was sentenced to fifty-one months in prison and ordered to pay $474,971 plus interest and penalties to the IRS.

Nobody *wants* to give the government 20 to 50 percent of their money, but Hatch's headline-making failure to pay his taxes is a staunch reminder that tax evasion will cost you much more in the long term than you're saving in the short term.

Since you are successful financially, taxes will be your biggest expense by a long shot. Taxes and tax strategy can quickly get complicated. While you can't eliminate taxes altogether, you can and should use every legal means to minimize their impact.

The tax code changes continually. If we went into depth on strategies here, it could be outdated before the ink on this page was dry. The US tax code is an absolute mess and nearly impossible for the average person to understand. I cannot stress that enough. There's no way I could even scratch the surface on the tax discussion in this book, but I can leave you with a couple of action items that will help you get your bearings in this dark and mysterious corner of your money galaxy.

First, you'll want to have a solid professional (or team of professionals) on your side. A good tax pro will help you know and play by the rules, help make the rules work for you, and will be worth many times what they cost.

Second, you'll want to communicate (or make sure your wealth management team communicates) with them before the most important tax deadline of the year—and it isn't April 15. Your most important tax deadline is December 31. If you don't communicate with your tax team until tax prep time in March or April, then you have a historian, not a strategist. At that point, there's not much the CPA can do. Since taxes are your biggest expense, you'll want to make sure you're doing everything you legally can to be a good steward of your wealth. That means there is communication late in the year—usually from late September to late October—so you know what the year looks like, with enough time left to make adjustments before your big tax deadline.

Last, from a tax perspective, your investments generally fall into one of three categories:

1. Taxable
2. Tax-Deferred
3. Tax-Free

Each category has its terms and conditions—stipulations, pros, and cons—so you'll probably want to diversify and have some in each category. How you do this should be coordinated and communicated with your team of professionals and coordinated with your overall plan.

REALITY #3: TIME

Time can work for you or against you. The Evil Clock, a villain I'll discuss in detail in the following chapter, is ticking all the time whether you look at it or not. It seems to *want* to get you off track. But time, unlike money, cannot be invested. There are no roll-over minutes and no bank to store them. Time is a commodity that can only be spent, and everyone has the same 168 hours in his or her week.

The actions and decisions we make day by day, week by week, year by year compound to create the life we have.

The Immutable Law of 168

As management guru Tom Peters said, "The calendar never, ever, ever lies."[9] They are 100 percent accurate and visible indicators of your priorities. In that vein, one of the most powerful principles I've encountered is the Immutable Law of 168.

The Immutable Law of 168 states: No matter how you "manage" your time, there are still only 168 hours in a week, and the quality of your life will be directly related to how you spend your 168 hours.

A recent Google search of *time management* found over 13.35 billion results. When we compare that to *Beyonce* (378 million results) and *Taylor Swift* (898 million results), we see that time management is a shockingly popular topic.

Dr. Terry O'Hara, who introduced the Immutable Law of 168 to me, asked, "Are there activities you need to rethink? Are there boundaries you need to establish? Are there things you need to get onto your calendar, or things you need to eliminate from your

168-hour week, to improve the quality of your life and the lives of the people you love? Do you spend time focusing on things beyond your control or on the things you can control? How will you spend your 168?"

Until we really crack the space-time continuum, we will be constrained to live within the limits of our 168 hours per week. The good news is … that's enough.

REALITY #4: THE FOUR LEVERS

Iron Man's extreme physical strength lies in his suit of armor. Tony Stark can cause the suit to fly, shoot projectiles, and create a force field. Just like Iron Man can flip switches and pull electronic levers to control his suit, you exercise that kind of power and control with your money.

There are plenty of factors you can't control, such as interest rates, the GDP growth rate, the political party in charge, geopolitical forces, inflation, deflation, and whether there will be another season of *Jersey Shore*. Spending time focusing on factors we cannot control is a fool's errand. But there are four levers you *can* pull to dramatically change the trajectory of your finances:

1. How you invest
2. How much you invest
3. How long you invest
4. How much you spend

The interplay of those four factors determines whether you'll become a financial superhero.

Lever 1: How You Invest

How you invest should be driven by your plan to achieve your goals. And there is no one right answer that works across the board. However, if you're investing for a long-term goal, you'll want to make sure you have long-term investments. If you're investing to pay your quarterly tax payment next quarter, you'll want to use safe, short-term investments. A money market is not even a passable investment for long-term investing, but it's a great instrument for liquidity and safety for short-term, known expenses.

Salespeople will find you. Many will try to convince you there's some big secret—the latest cash-value life insurance angle, virtual reality, or a crypto play no one else has figured out yet. You'll be better off staying away from those amateurs and sticking with proven, reliable investment vehicles like ownership in companies, such as stocks, stock funds, and private equity, or real assets like real estate.

Lever 2: How Much You Invest

When I got serious about building my own wealth, I ran the numbers and discovered I needed to invest more money each month than I was making. It was daunting. And so I created a schedule based on how much I could invest at that time and how much I would need to invest in future years in order to get on track. I started with a monthly commitment of $513 to an investment in addition to my 401(k). Why $513? Because that was all I could afford. Some months, it was a serious stretch. Today, that investment pays me thousands of dollars each year. If you're not spending income from your investments already, you can do the same thing. Start with what you can do.

Lever 3: How Long You Invest

The compounding effect is tremendous—but it relies on time. The more time you have before needing income, the more flexibility you have. Sometimes even a handful of years can make a huge difference. Delaying withdrawals not only gives you more time for your money to grow but you'll also have less time that your money needs to generate yield for your living expenses. It will put less stress on your portfolio.

If you've already arrived where you want to be asset-wise—great. Now is the time to make sure you stay in the position you want. If you're not there, get a plan to make it happen.

And let's be clear about longevity, or how long we should expect to live and therefore how long we'll need our money to last.

My team and I hear it all the time: "What is life expectancy these days? I probably won't live past my early eighties." Oddly, the person saying this usually has parents or grandparents in their midnineties!

The concept of "old age" is relative. Remember when you were twelve and your thirty-two-year-old schoolteacher seemed positively ancient? "Old" always seems to be twenty or thirty years older than we are right now. Until we get there. Then, it doesn't feel that old at all!

I'll tell you what I tell my clients: Plan on needing your money to last at least until age one hundred. That way, you're much more likely to have what you need for as long as you need it. Sure, that means you may die at eighty-five with some money in the bank, but that's okay. It's always better to have money and not need it than to need it and not have it.

Lever 4: How Much You Spend

It may sound strange, but most first-gen wealth families we work with do not have a budget. Budgeting is a great discipline—and most people need to budget when they're starting out financially and trying to figure out what kind of lifestyle works with their income. But in all my years watching people build wealth over time, I've seen that when people get in the habit of living a certain lifestyle *well below their income*, a budget isn't necessary. They live a post-budget lifestyle in a post-budget world.

How much is okay to spend and how much should you invest while you're still in accumulation mode? Your goals will determine that. Depending on when you get started, what your goals are, and other factors, we usually see saving and investing in the 10 to 30 percent of income range. If you're saving only 10 percent, that's on the lower end of the scale. If you've built a business that you'll be selling that represents the lion's share of your net worth, 10 percent may be plenty. If you started saving and investing late in life and have big goals and only recently started making a healthy income, you may be in the 30 percent or higher club.

It's not really about the money. It's not about the income. I've known people who made less than $100,000 per year who were wealthy and lived a post-budget life. And I've known people who consistently made more than $1,000,000 every year who spend more than they make and are stressed out, not saving enough, and essentially poor. It's about the decisions we make with the money we have. No matter your situation, there is something positive you can do.

Jim Rohn said, "Poor people spend their money and save what's left. Rich people save their money and spend what's left."[10] He espoused the 70/10/10/10 principle. Essentially, learn to live on 70 percent of your after-tax income. The remaining 30 percent should be divided in thirds among charitable giving, saving, and investing. Whether they heard that from Jim Rohn or not, that's exactly what most of our clients have done—at least at some point in their lives. Targeting a saving and investing rate of 20 percent or more is common for first-gen wealth during the accumulation years.

People who have practiced living off a fraction of their earnings, whether they are living off 70 percent or 50 percent (or less!) of their income, have constructed their lives in such a way that they can live a post-budget life.

What about when you start living off the portfolio— how much should you spend then? Your age, the age of your spouse if you have one, whether you're intent on leaving an inheritance, your health situation, and many other factors play into how to structure your income. I can, however, give some guidelines to help.

If you start living off your portfolio by age sixty-five, not only do you need to plan for that money to last for forty more years, you'll need to plan for your income to triple (or more) during your lifetime. Why triple? Because prices tend to go up over time. In 1995, a gallon of gas cost $1.15, a postage stamp cost $0.32, and the median home price was $106,000. If you start living off your portfolio before age sixty-five, you need to plan on at least tripling your income over your lifetime.

Plan to spend less than 5 percent of your assets when you start taking income. Why less than 5 percent? If you earn 6 or 8 or 20 percent, and you're spending less than 5 percent, you are building in future raises and creating a margin of safety. Spending only 3 percent is even better.

ROBERT THE RICH

I began working with Robert in the late 1990s. He was a quiet man, single, never married, simple in his tastes, and enjoyed photography, kayaking, and hiking. Plus, he spent time every week helping his parents who lived to the ages of ninety-nine and one hundred one.

If you measure wealth by raw dollars, Robert was very middle class. However, if you measure wealth by having more income than you spend each year, which is how he measured it, he was very wealthy.

The remarkable thing about Robert was that, at the apex of his career as an insurance adjuster, he earned only $36,000. And yet he had managed to pay off his modest house in Williamson County, Tennessee; pay cash for his Toyota; and maximize his IRA contributions each year. When he retired early at age fifty-one, he got more income from dividends on his portfolio than he ever earned in a year. When I asked him if he needed more income, his response was, "This income lets me do everything I want to do." In fact, by the time he started taking Social Security distributions, he was again saving and investing more money. Robert figured out the fourth lever.

He understood that every dollar was discretionary, and he exercised his sense of autonomy, agency, and control over the utility of money. He understood Lever #4.

REALITY #5: YOUR BIGGEST PROBLEM

The good news is that you can fix your biggest problem.

The bad news is that your biggest problem... is you.

And no matter where you go, there you are.

That really is good news. As a business coach told me, "If your biggest problem is you, then you can fix it. You can do what you need to do to get the outcome you want. You have agency, control; you're the boss of you. You are not a tree; your feet aren't planted. You can move, change, adjust, adapt. You may decide that you don't want to do anything differently, and that's okay. That's up to you."

LUKE—A HISTORY OF CARS

At thirty-one years old, Luke was recruited to a firm with the promise of better resources, better technology, and a six-figure signing bonus in addition to his six-figure income.

The first day in the new office, the branch manager encouraged him to cut loose, have some fun, buy a new house, get a new Mercedes or Lexus, and spend the bonus. One of the men in the office, a member of a prestigious country club, took a few jabs at Luke's "look."

"Where'd you get that suit? Men's Warehouse? You need to step up your game. Did you get those shoes at Shoe Carnival?"

In fact, Luke did buy his dress shoes at Shoe Carnival.

When his coworker found out what kind of car Luke drove, he wondered aloud if Luke had bought his *car* from Shoe Carnival as well.

Luke parked his nine-year-old Chrysler K car in his parking space between a Lexus and a Mercedes. He'd paid $2,300 for it. Even though Luke was a "car guy" whose father had owned a used car dealership, he couldn't bring himself to spend more than two weeks' earnings on a vehicle. As successful as he was in his career, he would be forty years old before he spent over $10,000 for a car.

In his early fifties, Luke's wife encouraged him to go out and buy what he referred to as a "stupid car." She said, "Look, you've been a car guy as long as I've known you and you've never spent much money on cars. We can do it now; it's not going to affect us financially. Why don't you go buy whatever you want?" And he did.

He loved the car and everything about it. Stepping into the car was more like *wearing* the car or putting the car on like a suit of clothes. It *fit*. It was an extension of his body. He loved the visceral feel of the road, the growl of the bi-turbo V8, the snap off the line as the wide, low-profile tires gripped the asphalt—all of which made his senses come to life. He loved driving that car.

And then a funny thing happened. He noticed that whenever he stopped at a stoplight, gas station, or got out of the car in a parking lot, people would talk to him about the car. They'd say, "What kind of car is it? It's beautiful." Young guys would rev their 5.0 Mustang engines.

It was a "look at me" car. That wasn't why he had wanted it. That wasn't why it had been his dream car. That wasn't why he bought it. He had no idea he would be so uncomfortable with the attention. Seven months later, he sold it and went back to a less noticeable, much less fun car—but one that was much more aligned with his values.

When his son heard the news, he asked, "Why would you ever sell that car? I thought you'd keep it forever." They had a conversation about the attention it drew and about the *utility of money*.

It was an opportunity to have a practical money conversation and share values with his son. They discussed what the car cost, the maintenance, and how much fun it was to drive. Then they discussed the things the family does together, what it costs, and the immense joy that brings. And while it wasn't an either/or proposition, the point was that the joy from having the car was a fraction of the joy he experienced from the things they do together. That money could bring more joy to Luke, his wife, and his son by doing something different with those dollars.

There is a reason the book *Think and Grow Rich* by Napoleon Hill has been a bestseller for so long. Wealth, in large part, has to do with mindset: What are you willing to do? Are you willing to forgo something today for a larger payoff tomorrow? Are you willing to do the work, build the skills, make the hard decisions that only you can make?

I think you're up to the task.

But first, you need to understand what you're up against, the dark forces that will inevitably rise against you as you try to take control of your financial superpowers and shape your money galaxy. In the next chapter, we'll identify the villains who want to get in our heads and get us off track, and then we'll cover strategies to get the results you want.

CHAPTER 5

THE SEVEN DEADLY FINANCIAL VILLAINS—PART 1

FROM MY EXPERIENCE, WHETHER YOU BELIEVE IN A cosmic fight between good and evil or not, there are villains that will show up regularly—with flair, style, and seduction—to do everything they can to derail you, throw you under the bus, and try to keep you from ever closing that gap between where you are now and your potential.

We will identify Seven Deadly Financial Villains who are out to destroy your wealth—or prevent you from ever building it in the first place. Before looking at strategies to overcome them, we will need to identify them, explore their origin stories, and understand how they attack us. I'll do just that over the next few chapters, starting here with the first three.

VILLAIN #1: THE EVIL CLOCK

The Evil Clock is one of the most insidious villains because he camouflages himself in a cloak woven with threads of logic. While not invisible, the Evil Clock can be quite difficult to spot.

Because Father Time waits for no one, his son, the young Clock, became angry at his father's lack of attention and began acting out. He spent his days convincing people they had plenty of time—so why get started today? As he deluded more and more people and still got no attention from his father, Clock crossed the line from angry to evil.

As people became more sophisticated, the Clock developed a more entangled ruse: Confuse people about what their "time horizon" is. Evil Clock loves convincing people that *time horizon* refers to the date they "retire" or start drawing income from their portfolio. But it's not. That is not the finish line. Their time horizon is how long the money needs to last. (Someone who is sixty years old and plans to retire in two years does not have a two-year time horizon; they likely have a forty-year time horizon.)

The only way to defeat the Evil Clock is by summoning your superpower of consistent execution to continue a smart game plan.

THE EVIL CLOCK STRIKES AT THE HORIZON

Late one Friday afternoon, while packing up my computer, phone, coffee cup, and keys, I fumbled to pick the phone up as it rang.

"Hey, I was just looking at my account, and I see that we hit my number!" Barry said in a sing-song voice before I could even say hello. "In fact, it's about fifty grand more than our target number. And two years early!"

"Yep, Barry. You've made smart choices along the way. I knew you and Olivia would get here," I replied.

Two years earlier, Barry sold the company he'd started and built. He agreed to stay on and work for the new owner for three years to help with the transition. In just a little more than a year, his main source of income would no longer be the company he'd owned. It would be the money that represented payment for his years of hard work.

"Well, we appreciate your help making those decisions and having the confidence to do some of the things we've done. But I have a question," Barry continued. "Shouldn't we just take everything out of the markets and put it in something really safe? I mean, with everything that's going on politically and with the economy and with the possibility of war, wouldn't it make sense to put all the money in something safe until the world is more stable? I mean, when you get to my age, you'll probably be thinking the same thing too. I probably shouldn't even buy green bananas anymore."

"Barry, you don't look a day over eighty-five."

"Hey, I'm only sixty-three!" We both chuckled at our dad jokes.

"I know you're going to tell me with your health and the history of the men in your family that you probably won't make it to age ninety or a hundred," I said. "But, Barry, here's what we have to figure out: Over the course of the next thirty, maybe forty years, how is Olivia going to double or triple her income? Let me pause a second for that to sink in."

As the idea set in for a few seconds, I continued, "I know that may sound audacious, so let's step into the Wayback Machine. How much was a postage stamp in 1996? It was $0.32. That same postage stamp in 2024 is $0.66. In twenty-eight years, the cost to send a letter has more than doubled. And bread, gas, and a trip to a restaurant, well, don't get me started. If Olivia lives to an age like her mom did, her income will need to double—and probably triple, or maybe even more. And I hope you're around, too, Barry."

"Triple?" Barry says, still letting it sink in.

"In that same time, from 1996 to 2024, the dividend on the S&P 500 more than quadrupled—and the growth has been even more than that," I said.* "The only rational hope for Olivia—and for you— to have the income you want, to do what you want to do, is to invest in the best of human ingenuity. By that I mean to invest in companies founded and run by some of the most innovative minds on the planet. Changing course and investing in something that may give you the income you need now but doesn't have the ability to double or triple in the next few decades just doesn't make sense."

Barry paused and said, "I think I get what you're saying. I had this number as a target to get to and we got there. Yeah. But it's not really the finish line, is it? It's just one more step in the journey. Does that sound right?"

"Exactly right."

"Okay. I'll go back to doing what I do, and you can get back to making sure I can do what I want to do—even when that postage stamp goes up to $1.32! It's easier for me to outsource the discipline to execute to you, and I can get on with Olivia's plans for me this weekend."

And with that, Barry summoned his inner financial superpowers for consistent execution of his plan to overcome the Evil Clock, because he understood that his *time horizon* is not his income start date but how long his money needs to last.

---

*In 1996, first-class US postage stamps were $0.32, and in 2024 they were $0.66. The 1996 dividend on SPY, an S&P 500–tracking Exchange Traded Fund, was $1.35 per share. In 2023, the dividend totaled $6.63 per share. The share price at the beginning of 1996 was approximately $63. In January of 2024, the share price was greater than $470. During that time, the S&P—and the funds that track it—suffered four major declines, including one in excess of -50 percent, two by more than -40 percent, and one in excess of -25 percent.

I find it interesting that our firm's two chronologically oldest clients continue to be very comfortable with having most of their money in equities. This flies in the face of conventional wisdom. The clients' logic is simple and effective. It goes something like this: The dividends produced by their portfolio are sufficient for most of their needs. They've been investing in equities for more than fifty years. Why would they relegate a sizable part of their portfolio to investments that probably will not even keep up with inflation?

That logic is . . . well . . . logical. When the stock market is exhibiting wiggles on the downside, those are the clients who often call to ask me and our team, "How are you doing? I know you know that this too shall pass. But I know it can be stressful for you sometimes when other people don't realize how the markets work." It's comforting to have clients in their nineties call to offer encouragement during times of volatility.

The best way to overcome the Evil Clock is with the Power of a Plan that aligns with your Power of Purpose.

The Evil Clock Strikes at the Compounding Effect

Since Sally was so mature for her age, she started babysitting when she was eleven years old. She loved kids and wanted to be a stay-at-home mom, so her parents encouraged her to start saving immediately. She put her money to work.

Steve, Sally's classmate, knew he wanted a red Mustang before he was even in elementary school. At age eleven, the same summer Sally started babysitting, he started mowing yards to buy that Mustang. Steve got the Mustang in high school, and after college, he began saving money for wealth-building at age twenty-five.

Both are serious about putting their money to work and both started relatively early. The Evil Clock was lurking, but both Sally and Steve were trying to make the most of the time they had.

How did they do?

Let's look at an example (hypothetical, of course, to keep the attorneys at bay). In this example, Sally and Steve are the same age and both earn exactly the same rate of return—7 percent annually. Both invest $1,000 per year. However, Sally starts investing at age eleven and invests $1,000 per year for *only* ten years, up to age twenty, for a total of $10,000 invested.

Steve waits until age twenty-five and invests $1,000 each year for the next forty-one years, until he turns sixty-five years old, for a total of $41,000 invested.

Age	Sally's year-end balance	Sally's cumulative investment	Steve's year-end balance	Steve's cumulative investment
11	$1,070	$1,000	$0	$0
25	$20,734	$10,000	$1070	$1,000
35	$40,788	$10,000	$16,888	$11,000
45	$80,237	$10,000	$48,006	$21,000
55	$157,838	$10,000	$109,218	$31,000
65	$310,492	$10,000	$229,632	$41,000

Again, Steve invested over *four times* more than Sally (his $41,000 compared to her $10,000), and they earned *the same* 7 percent return. But look at what they've got at age sixty-five. Steve has $229,632 in his account, while Sally, who hasn't added anything to her investments for the past forty-five years, is sitting on $310,492. She earned *35 percent more money* than Steve, even though she contributed 75 percent less money than he did!

That's the power of compounding over time.

The Evil Clock knows about the Time Lever, how it affects the power of compounding, and how powerful it can be. And that mean ol' Clock just loves stealing your potential wealth by convincing you that you've got plenty of time before you "have to worry about investing."

You may not be eleven years old today, but you're absolutely closer to eleven years old today than you will be tomorrow. And if you have kids, they're certainly closer to eleven years old than you are! Just think how powerful this lesson could be for them if they "got it" that early!

The only way to defeat the Evil Clock is to summon your superpower of consistent execution of your plan to get started immediately.

VILLAIN #2: THE LEVER DENIER

The next villain is LD, short for the Lever Denier. LD's father was a denier. You name it, he probably denied it. He was a round earth denier. If science was observation, he'd argue, then just observe the horizon. See? It's obvious that the earth is flat. If the earth were round and rotating, people would go flying off. That's the real law of physics.

Don't go down that old hoax about "the law of gravity," either. Can you prove gravity? Of course you can't.

And if the moon landing had actually happened, rather than being filmed in a Hollywood basement, those photos wouldn't have stripes on them. Clearly, those pictures were doctored.

He even denies the immutable law of Six Degrees of Kevin Bacon!

LD grew up hearing his dad debunk all these so-called truths and facts. How could you live your whole life in that environment and not have it rub off? It did. But like most sons, at some point, LD decided he didn't want to be exactly like his father. So he decided to focus on denying the Four Levers (how you invest, how much you invest, how long you invest, and how much you spend).

He shows up on social media, at cocktail parties, and networking events. He's attractive, unoffensive, and has a mysterious air about him. He works diligently and with seeming logic. His shifts are subtle, so it's not obvious when he makes shifts in logic.

For Lever One, how you invest, LD always comes up with a theme that sounds plausible. You should become your own banker. The entire banking system is a conspiracy "they" came up with to keep you down. All his really smart clients are using the latest insurance policy that builds cash value, only goes up and never goes down in value, and even walks your dog and waters your petunias. He also discovered the secret to crypto that most people don't know about yet because "they" are keeping it a secret. But he can get you in on it.

For Lever Two, how long you invest, he tries to steer clear of the whole *compound interest* conversation. The best he can do is point out that Einstein said compound interest was one of the wonders of the world, and we all know that Einstein's theories have largely been debunked by quantum mechanics. (But don't start down the science road, because then he'll have to talk about the shape of the earth.)

For Lever Three, how much you invest, he'll simply taunt you with numbers he believes are just out of your reach. But as a favor, he could accommodate someone like you in one of his get-rich-quick deals. Simply because he likes you.

For Lever Four, how much you spend, he will likely deny that spending is an issue at all. In fact, he will quickly shift the conversation to what you can spend money on rather than how much money you can spend each year.

The most successful way to overcome LD is through the Power of a Plan aligned with your Power of Purpose and consistent execution. He is no match for the combination of those three powers.

VILLAIN #3: FINANCIAL PORNOGRAPHY (FINPORN)

According to *Merriam-Webster*, thousands of new words are created every year. In fact, in just one recent month, September 2023, six hundred and ninety words were added to our dictionary. However, not all of those are used enough and widespread enough to stick around.

I propose a new addition to our language (along the lines of FinTech): *FinPorn*. No, this doesn't refer to pornography from the country of Finland but rather what I would call *financial pornography*.

The dictionary entry would look something like this:

FinPorn [fin-porn]

noun

1. the depiction of financially explicit charts, graphs, videos, photographs, or the like, whose purpose is to elicit financial arousal.

    a: In particular, images involving overweight, balding, middle-aged men or women, fully clothed, wearing professional attire and frequently donning tortoiseshell reading glasses or black-rimmed librarian glasses.

    b: material (such as books or analyst reports) that depict behavior intended to cause financial excitement.

    c: the depiction of acts in a manner so as to arouse a quick, intense emotional reaction relating to money, which can include TikTok and YouTube videos promising to show you the "secret"— for a *small* fee.

Of the Seven Deadly Financial Villains out to destroy your wealth (or prevent you from ever building it in the first place), FinPorn (aka Finn) is one of the most attractive, polished, and hardest to resist.

She inherited her parents' obsession with money. Her ADD caused her to move rapidly from one topic to another. Finn studied economics and business and wrote her thesis on plausible yet unconfirmed and unsubstantiated economic ideas and theories. Her trade involves data and information.

Information can lead to insight, which can lead to knowledge and wisdom. Finn prefers to live in the data and information realm.

Information is random, chaotic, and miscellaneous. Knowledge, on the other hand, is orderly, cumulative, and focused. Finn relies on randomness, chaos, and *miscellaneousness*. (Hey, look! I made up yet another word!)

When we analyze media companies, we find that most magazines, TV programs, newspapers, websites, YouTube channels, and radio shows have a common business model. Their income is derived from advertising revenue. It's a simple equation: The more eyeballs watching, the more valuable the advertisement space. How do you get eyeballs? Media outlets tap into the emotion of fear and the hot button of aspiration and provide *information* but not *insight* or wisdom.

One segment sells fear because the markets are about to crash, but after a short commercial break, "Don't miss our next guest, who will tell us why you won't want to miss out because the market is about to take off to the upside." The magazine headline story focuses on avoiding loss. But the smaller headings focus on aspiration or greed. "Where should you invest for profits over the next few weeks? Find out from our experts. You can't retire without these secrets. Don't touch that dial. We'll be back after a short commercial break. Be sure to tune in to the show tomorrow."

This is not an indictment of all media, or *any* media, for that matter. It really has to do with how we consume the information and what we intend to do with the information.

The Crystal Gall

Our brains crave certainty and are working all the time to predict the future. In fact, where information is missing, our minds do a remarkable job of making stuff up to fill in the unknown. Don't believe me? Think back to the last time you weren't able to get in touch with someone you care deeply about—a spouse, child, parent, grandparent, or friend. It doesn't take long before we begin to imagine their overturned car stuck in a ditch, their aging body sprawled on the kitchen floor with a broken hip, or their cries for help as they're tied up and carried off by rampaging pirates. Finn takes this concept—this human desire for certainty—and perverts it.

Ancient Greeks had a particular disdain for hubris. Their stories of the gods taking revenge on prideful men abound. Sadly, pride is just as prevalent today as it was in Homer's mythical Greek tales, and we are neck-deep in financial fortune tellers' lies.

You hear it in narratives where people have the gall to have a crystal ball, to pretend to know the future. "China is going to . . ." "Russia is going to . . ." "The Fed is going to . . ." You see these predictions from Nobel Prize–winning economists in the popular press, even though these economists have been worse at predicting the demise of the internet or the probability of the next recession than a Vegas gambler.

I've kept a book in my office as a reminder for several decades. It's by a Nobel Prize–winning economist who is still a professor at a prominent university. The book is about surviving the coming Great Depression that will, without a doubt, occur in 1988. Or 1989.

Still waiting.

In reality, the Dow Jones Industrial Average has gone up more than fifteenfold since that book's publication. This disparity between the author's "guaranteed" depression and the Dow's massive gains points to the truth of the statement: If you took all the economists in the world and laid them end-to-end, you still couldn't reach a conclusion. It also points to a statement made several times by Peter Lynch, one of the most successful mutual fund managers of all time. He said he never listened to what economists said, because listening to economists never helped him make money. He just looked for good investments.

Nowhere is hubris more evident than the "shouldn't be here" statements. They sound something like this: "The markets shouldn't be this high; they are way overvalued." Or, "This stock shouldn't be this low; it's a great value." But let's stop for a moment and break down those kinds of statements. There is one person telling us the world shouldn't be the way it is. And maybe, in their minds, it shouldn't be that way.

And yet... it is.

These prideful fortune tellers are saying, in essence, that reality *shouldn't be* what reality *is*.

Tell me... who is the madman? We usually reserve that title for crazy people who deny reality.

This is the reason why, when people ask me where the stock market or interest rates will be a year from now, my answer is always a polite version of *I don't know*. I've never known. I never will know. Neither does anyone else. The great news is that I don't *have* to know in order to make good decisions. That's not a sales pitch for certainty or having the gall to sell a crystal ball story; it's just the truth.

And, you know, I have found truth to be infinitely freeing.

Unlike Finn, who uses Crystal Gall and other mythological creatures.

Black Swans and Sea Monsters

Prior to their discovery by a Dutch explorer in 1697, black swans were a bird no one thought possible and something that simply didn't exist. For years, all swans were thought to be white. That was all that had ever been reported.

FinPorn loves the fear of black swans. She uses her unsubstantiated-yet-plausible-sounding economic theories to create fear about yet-unseen *black swan events* (aka BS events). But the fear of a BS event is like the fear of sea monsters lurking below the water's surface, like stealthy sharks circling beneath unsuspecting swimmers. These fears can divert attention, create havoc, and ignite chaos.

The Financial Crisis of 2008 (or "the investing opportunity of a lifetime of 2008," as it should more aptly be called) was an example of a black swan event. And yet the laws of supply and demand held pat. It would appear that, at least from my experience, the fear of black swan and sea monster attacks that never occur causes more damage and havoc than the attacks themselves. The sad reality is that just the fear of events that ultimately never happened has erased the wealth of many families.

WARREN'S NOT LOOKING BACK

Warren has owned several businesses and built a robust consulting business, earning him a steady six-figure income. His wife is a successful healthcare executive earning an even healthier six-figure income. This is a second marriage for him, and she is significantly younger than him. Warren has adult children from his first marriage, and because of their blended family situation, the two had always kept their finances separate. Despite being fully committed to their marriage, the couple had a prenuptial agreement, they still filed separate tax returns, they kept all their accounts separate, and they didn't even share access to online account portals.

Warren met with my team largely because of his wife's concern about the "relationship" Warren had with FinPorn years before. Finn got to him during a particularly busy time in his career in early 2009, and via the seductive urging of market pundits and experts, Finn had convinced him to convert his entire portfolio to "safe" investments. When Warren came to see us in early 2023, he was still invested in money market instruments.

Finn had been able to use the fear of a black swan event to prevent Warren from participating in a market that had gone up substantially while he kept his head—and his money—buried in the sand. From April 2009 through February 2023, the S&P went up more than fourfold, and Warren missed out on all that wonderful growth.

Through hard work and financial counseling, Warren managed to break his addiction to Finn and refocused on his business and family. It was hard for him, though, to think about what he'd missed. We encouraged him to look at where he is now, the substantial wealth he has, and the fact that he now has a plan that is being consistently executed.

"You know what they say: The best time to plant a tree was thirty years ago," he mused. "But the second-best time to plant is right now. I just need to stay focused on that and the work that I love doing."

The best way to overcome Finn is to invoke all three of the superpowers: Power of Purpose, Power of Plan, and Power of Execution. Staying focused on the disciplined execution of the plan with the true north of the Power of Purpose will allow you to overcome her distractions.

You may find that Financial Pornography, the Lever Denier, and the Evil Clock often work in alliances with other financial villains. But regardless of whether you face them one at a time or in an onslaught of multiples, you can live confidently in the knowledge that your financial superpowers are all you need to consistently emerge victorious.

Now let's meet the next two of the Seven Deadly Financial Villains we need to be aware of before delving into specific strategies to overcome them.

CHAPTER 6

THE SEVEN DEADLY FINANCIAL VILLAINS—PART 2

I N THE PREVIOUS CHAPTER, WE EXPLORED THE THREE deceitful and dastardly villains who are working against your financial success. In this chapter, we'll continue the discussion by examining the next two money crooks, the no-good, rotten Jones brothers: Brother Keeping-Up-With-The and his snooty sibling, Brother Dow.

VILLAIN #4: THE JONES BROTHERS: BROTHER KEEPING-UP-WITH-THE

The Jones Brothers Gang rides roughshod over destroyed wealth. The gang includes both Brother Dow and his older brother, Keeping-Up-With-The, whom everyone calls KUWT (pronounced *Coot*). The gang has been doing their part to destroy your wealth (or prevent you from ever building it in the first place) your entire life.

Theodore Roosevelt is credited with having said, "Comparison is the thief of joy." Whether by culture or by design, our brains seem to move toward a sense of comparison quite handily. We humans are social creatures and instinctively seem to notice how we're doing relative to those around us. And it's not always trying to get way ahead of others; sometimes just fitting in and keeping up is good enough.

Humans are not the only creatures in the animal kingdom that have developed ways of signaling status. Just as peacocks signal to peahens that they are worthy mates by showing off their amazing tail feathers, humans have their own signaling. Instead of feathers, humans often use clothing, automobiles, vacations, watches, surgery, and real estate to display status. It works.

THE GREENS

It was a sunny afternoon when the Greens drove up in a special edition BMW 5-Series. The couple came into the office together.

A mutual friend had asked me if I would meet with them as a favor. He said he knew they may not be what my team and I typically deal with, but maybe we could help.

We settled into a brief conversation and then began the Wealth Roadmap. It went fine and they were clear about what was important to them.

"You can see, the main thing is that we need to reduce stress. Maybe you can figure out how to arrange things, because it shouldn't be this stressful," Katy Green pled.

Mark Green nodded in agreement and added, "I just want her to be happy."

When we got to their numbers, it was clear where the stress was coming from. Feeling like Captain Obvious, I said, "You're spending a lot more than you're making. You've spent most of your savings. What's going on?"

"We're just living like our friends and neighbors," Katy replied. "In fact, we don't go on vacations like most of them do. We're just living a normal life."

Their mortgage alone was a huge percentage of their income. I asked about the car.

"It's a lease. The lease is up next month," Katy said.

"That's great. So that's right at $1,000 per month that goes away."

"No," she sighed. "The lease on the new one will be about $150 per month more."

"Katy, you're having trouble paying your mortgage, you have large credit card bills, and your savings is almost gone," I countered. "You can't afford the car on what you two are making. It just doesn't work."

"You don't understand. We can't have kids. I always wanted kids," she began crying. "A nice car is the one luxury I allow myself. I think I deserve it. It's one luxury that helps me forget. I mean, we don't go on vacation. Sure, we go out to eat at nice restaurants, but so do our friends. We can't just stay at home. And that car is the one luxury I have because we are childless."

My heart broke for them. I can't know the pain she faced. That's a trial I don't have to face.

They left that day a little sad—not because I couldn't arrange things to magically make a negative cash flow work, but because I hadn't been able to convince them that they had agency and power. They had everything they needed to change their situation, but they couldn't get to the point of believing in their own potential.

Unfortunately and predictably, they lost their house to the bank and had the new leased car taken away. No winners in that story.

While this is a severe story, it plays out many times.

A close friend that owns several high-end car dealerships told me he sees people come in all the time buying a car he knows they can't afford. His sales team even tries to talk people out of buying when they realize the customer is trying to use a new car to "scratch an itch that just can't be scratched." Even professional salespeople understand that retail therapy doesn't soothe every wound.

If you get right down to it, trying to keep up with the Joneses doesn't work because the Jones clan is trying to keep up with the Smiths who are trying to keep up with the Williamsons, and they don't have any idea what they're doing.

Studies have shown we would rather have less in absolute terms as long as we're doing better in relative terms to those around us. One study cited in Dan Ariely's book *Predictably Irrational* showed that most participants would rather have a lower absolute income as long as they made more than their peers than to have a much higher income that was less than their peers. This illustrates how susceptible we are to the social influence of what others are doing.

ORDINARY SUPERSTAR

In the midnineties, I had a client who was a successful songwriter and music producer. He wrote songs played on pop, country, and Christian radio and produced songs played across the country each Christmas season. Anyone in the US over the age of twelve would be familiar with his work.

This guy drove a modest car he purchased used, and he wore a cheap watch. He usually wore Levi's, tennis shoes, and a T-shirt. He is a great guy: completely unpretentious, a family man, a caring father and husband, and active in the community. He is the kind of guy who has plenty of good friends and keeps them for decades. You can't find anyone to say a bad thing about him.

When we first started working together in the midnineties, we reviewed his tax returns. He'd had only two years over the previous decade when he made less than $800,000 (but those years were still over $500,000). That was some seriously serious money back in the day. A couple of weeks into our financial advisory relationship, he called because he got a tax bill from his CPA that he wasn't expecting. He was going to owe $54,000.

"I'm trying to figure out what to do. We don't have the money, and it's due to the IRS. Do we have anywhere we can pull it from?" he asked on the phone, stress in his voice.

"Everything we just took over is in retirement accounts. If you pull it from there, you'll have a penalty plus more tax to pay. What about your reserves? We just talked about a line of credit—have you established that yet?" I asked.

"No. I'll have to go to the bank and see if they'll loan me some money," he said.

He managed to get a bank loan quick enough to pay the urgent tax bill, but I was left with some big questions about what had happened—questions

I felt would be better handled face-to-face. So, we met a couple of weeks later to dig into how he'd gotten into that mess.

I opened the meeting by saying, "I'm trying to figure out what's going on with your cash flow. For example, I see you're spending a little over $4,000 a month on 'food.' And that does not include eating out. Can you help me understand this?"

We looked at the itemized expenses together. "Oh, oh yeah. That's on Barb's card. That's stuff for the kids like Starbucks in the morning on the way to school and after school, like ice cream or frozen yogurt," he said.

"Wait, that's just snacks?" I asked.

"Yeah. I mean it's not like they're going to a fancy steakhouse every day. Kids are hungry after school. And if they have a group of friends with them, we take care of that too. We think it's important to be generous."

"And what about this card? It looks like it's more eating out?" I asked.

"Yeah. That's mine. Like here, I was doing a session in London, and then I met up with Mutt Lange and we went out for dinner a couple of nights. That's never cheap, but that's just part of the business."

I looked at this man who was driving a $20,000 unpretentious car and wearing a cheap watch, T-shirt, and old Levi's, making $1 million a year and having nothing to show for it.

I felt like a failure. For three years I tried. I spoke with his CPA and management companies. They both were getting ready to stop working with him. We couldn't make any headway on setting up systems and an environment for him to be successful. When it came time for retirement plan contributions, he didn't have the money. When it came time for quarterly tax payments, it was a scramble, despite his robust income.

Finally, I confronted the situation and told him that if we can't make a difference in his life, then we'd need to disengage and see if we could find someone who was better suited to help.

The music business has changed dramatically in the years since then. His checks still show up, but they're much smaller now. He and his family have had to downsize dramatically and learn to live in a smaller home, on a reduced income.

If we take our eyes off our true benchmark—our *own* benchmark, the one that is set up with the Wealth Roadmap—it's easy to try to fit into something we don't really, at our core, want.

Money has a way of trying to be the boss. It wants to bully us. A musician client once told me, "When you get to a certain point, you have to be careful. Because if you're not, the truth is you don't own your stuff. Your stuff owns you."

The most effective first-gen wealth strategy I've observed is using the Power of Purpose—reconnecting with our deep why and the magnetic vision of the future—to counteract this tendency all of us seem to possess to one degree or another. KUWT is very adept at keeping us focused on what others want and have rather than on what each of us wants and has ourselves. His power of distraction is legendary.

VILLAIN #5: THE JONES BROTHERS: BROTHER DOW

Brother Dow, the younger and more intelligent of the brothers, works diligently under the cloak of intellectualism to take unwary victims to the poorhouse. To overcome him, we must first understand him; and to understand him, we must first understand the *market index*. We'll dive in for a moment to provide some background on market indexes since they are mentioned in virtually every online forum, news feed, and in the nightly news. They are also the primary tool Brother Dow uses as a distraction to get you off track.

What Is an Index?

A market index, such as the S&P 500, the Dow Jones Industrial Index, or the Nasdaq Composite, is a collection of investments with a specific criterion for selection.

Let's start with the Dow Jones Industrial Average (aka *the Dow*) as an example. There is a committee that selects thirty companies to represent the US economy. The index is *price-weighted*, meaning the companies with the highest stock price have the most impact on the index. (There is a formula for adjusting for stock splits, which affect price. Because of this, the formula is now many pages long.)

The S&P 500, on the other hand, is *capitalization-weighted*, meaning the bigger companies have more influence on the index. It's akin to the House of Representatives—but instead of more population equaling more votes, more overall stock value (market capitalization) equals more votes. There is significant difference in the impact the big companies have compared to the small because of capitalization weighting.

In fact, as of February 2024, the smallest 469 companies have *less* influence on the index than the largest thirty-four. Said another way, the largest thirty-four companies in the S&P 500 have more impact on the index than all the rest of the stocks in the index. (Yes, that adds up to 503 stocks in the S&P, but that is the correct number because of spinoffs.) If the largest thirty-four stocks move up 1 percent and all the other 469 go down 1 percent, the S&P will still be up.

The Nasdaq Composite is also capitalization-weighted. Its stocks typically don't pay much in terms of dividends. Dow Jones Industrial Average stocks tend to pay higher dividends than the S&P 500, and the S&P pays higher dividends than the Nasdaq. (It's important to note that the Dow Jones Industrial Average, like most indexes, has changed over the years and now includes large companies that trade on the Nasdaq exchange.)

Why does it work that way? It's arbitrary. It's the way the index creator said it would be. The indexes created by our wealth management firm work differently. Why? It's arbitrary. We created our indexes with different selection and weighting criteria.

What Is the Purpose of an Index?
Indexes provide a benchmark for performance. They are often (maybe usually) created to promote something. To be clear, indexes are usually created to *sell* something.

For example, Charles Dow created the Dow Jones Industrial Average Index in 1885 to promote his fledgling publication he called the *Wall Street Journal*. The index was an easy way to communicate the general direction of stocks.

The Nasdaq Composite Index was created to highlight the performance of the Nasdaq companies relative to other indexes in order to encourage and entice investors to invest in the kinds of companies listed on the Nasdaq—which are typically smaller, newer, and innovative—as opposed to stodgy, old Blue Chip–type companies found in the Dow Jones Industrial Average and that, historically, traded on the New York Stock Exchange.

When the wealth management firm I started wanted to share our unique investment strategies, we launched indexes that were calculated by S&P Dow Jones (the two companies are now one). Having a stock index allowed investment firms to easily view the performance of the strategies we created and helped the fund we managed using those strategies leapfrog the approval process that got many firms stuck. The existence of our indexes allowed us to promote, or *sell*, our process.

But Which Market Index Should We Use?

This is where Brother Dow gets his kicks. Sometimes the Dow outperforms the Nasdaq. Sometimes the Nasdaq outperforms the S&P and the Dow. Sometimes the Barclays Aggregate Bond Index outperforms the S&P. Sometimes the Emerging Markets Index outperforms all US indexes. When the indexes seem to point different directions, the reasonable question becomes, *Which one should we use?*

Over the past thirty-plus years, Brother Dow has worked his dastardly deeds of distraction by making sure there have been years on end in which people wanted to use the Dow as their benchmark—until people stopped caring about the Dow and just wanted to know how they were doing relative to the Nasdaq. That lasted until about mid-2000, when interest in the Nasdaq fell off a cliff. No one asked about the Nasdaq as a benchmark for the next decade and a half. (The Nasdaq 100 didn't get back to its 2000 high until about 2017. A buy-and-hold investor in the Nasdaq in early 2000 would've had a negative return for sixteen-plus years.) Then they cared about international markets—until they didn't. During market downturns, like the COVID Contraction in 2020 or 2022 as recent examples, focus comes off market indexes and shifts to absolute returns. The question simply became, Did I make any money (or at least not lose very much)?

This vacillation from one index to another is exactly the kind of tail-chasing that Brother Dow does his downright darndest to use to derail us from our destination.

The Most Important Benchmark

The most important benchmark is *your* index, the *You Index*. How are you tracking toward reaching your goals for your reasons?

Brother Dow tries to get you to forget that. He tries to get you to think your job is to keep up with one index or another, changing from one index to a completely different one with regularity. Like a game of index whack-a-mole. And he often works in conjunction with FinPorn to destroy you financially.

But the reality is that it doesn't make a difference if you outperform one index or another if you don't reach your goals. What if the market is down 5 percent and you're down 4 percent? You outperformed the index. Do you declare victory? The question is, Did that get you to your goal? Or if one index is up 10 percent and you're up 11 percent but you underfunded the goal so there's no hope in you actually achieving it, is that a victory? Brother Dow will try to convince you it is.

His job is to get you to take your eyes off what matters.

This takes us back to the Power of Plan—your plan that is focused on reaching your goals and hitting your benchmarks and milestones along the way. Are you on track for your goals? If not, what adjustments do you (not Brother Dow) need to make?

Good news! You've made it this far and you're almost through meeting the villains and understanding the forces pitted against your success.

Prepare for the last two. They may be the headiest of the criminal crew.

CHAPTER 7

THE SEVEN DEADLY FINANCIAL VILLAINS—PART 3

AS WE DIVE INTO OUR LAST TWO VILLAINS, LET'S KEEP in mind that the point of identifying them is to have a framework to recognize them so we can evict them from our lives. Despite the pervasiveness and determined desire of the villains, the three core superpowers will help you stay on the track of financial success as you've defined it.

VILLAIN #6: MARKET MATH

Market Math, or *Double M* as the kids at school called him, was the intellectual nerd who never fit in. Logical and intelligent, he grew bitter about being an outcast and learned to use his brain to make subtle shifts in logic and obscure the truth with statistics to manipulate people. He's a miserable fella, but he manages to find at least a little joy in one of the few ways he can, by engineering the misfortune of others.

Double M loves to quote Mark Twain (who attributed the quote to Benjamin Disraeli): "There are three kinds of lies: lies, damned lies, and statistics." Reciting this personal mantra to himself always brings a wry smile to his face, but he never reveals the reason behind that smile.

Using his favorite tools to derail wealth always brings Double M pleasure—it is affirmation that he is smart and can manipulate unsuspecting minds.

Here are some of the strategies Double M uses.

The Inequality of Gains and Losses

Losses hurt. Not only is the subjective emotional pain excruciating but the objective financial losses make recovery difficult. Behavioral finance and psychology have taught us that *loss aversion*, fueled by fear, is a much stronger emotion than the aspirational *desire for gain*. That is, we're more motivated by not losing something we already have than we are about gaining something new. The math of gains and losses supports this hardwired thinking.

Suppose you had an investment that *lost* 10 percent one year and *made* 10 percent the next. You started with $100,000 and lost 10 percent, leaving you with $90,000. Then you made 10 percent, leaving you not with your original $100,000 but with $99,000. That's 1 percent less than you started with. When you're dealing with percentages, losing ten and gaining ten doesn't even out; it leaves you with a loss. You'd need a gain of *more* than *11 percent* to make up for that *10 percent loss*.

But wait, it gets worse.

The larger the loss, the greater the subsequent recovery must be to break even. For example, a 20 percent loss requires a 25 percent gain; a 30 percent loss requires a 43 percent gain; and a 40 percent loss requires a 67 percent gain to get back to where you started.

If Your Portfolio Lost...	Gains Needed to Break Even	The Time It Takes to Get Back to Even at 3%	The Time It Takes to Get Back to Even at 6%
10%	11%	3.6 yrs.	1.8 yrs.
20%	25%	7.5 yrs.	3.8 yrs.
30%	43%	11.9 yrs.	6 yrs.
40%	67%	17 yrs.	8.6 yrs.
50%	100%	23.2 yrs.	11.6 yrs.

Let's take this a step further. Consider the drop in the Nasdaq in the early 2000s (2000–2002), and say an investor with $100,000 experienced a 75 percent loss of value one year, followed by a 75 percent gain the next year. How much do you think she'd have when the dust settled the second year? Close to even? Down 10 percent? Down 20 percent?

Not even close.

In this situation, the investor would be down more than 56 percent. Her $100,000 investment would have taken a 75 percent decline followed by a matching 75 percent recovery, leaving her with $44,000 of her original $100,000.

Gains and losses are not created equal.

We can almost hear the villainous Market Math snickering.

The Inequality of Gains:
Not All 10 Percent Gains Are the Same

When we look at "average" rates of return, it should be helpful to remember the following table that illustrates three different portfolios. Consistent returns and compounding can have a dramatic impact on investments over time. Even though the average return is the same for all four portfolios after twenty years—it is 10 percent—how the returns are achieved adds up to a difference of more than $53,000 on an initial investment of $100,000.

The Value of $100,000 Invested

Year	Portfolio A	Portfolio B	Portfolio C
1	10%	7%	20%
2	10%	13%	20%
3	10%	7%	20%
4	10%	13%	20%
5	10%	7%	20%
6	10%	13%	20%
7	10%	7%	20%
8	10%	13%	20%
9	10%	7%	20%
10	10%	13%	20%
11	10%	7%	0%
12	10%	13%	0%
13	10%	7%	0%
14	10%	13%	0%
15	10%	7%	0%
16	10%	13%	0%
17	10%	7%	0%
18	10%	13%	0%
19	10%	7%	0%
20	10%	13%	0%
Average Return	10%	10%	10%
Value	$672,750	$667,763	$619,174

This table is for illustrative purposes only and is not meant to predict or indicate future performance. Past performance doesn't mean jack.

This is one of the ways Market Math messes with investors. But he'll always take it a step further. Suppose you can make an investment that you plan on using in five years, and you have a choice of account A or B. In this example, you also know what the returns will be in advance. Account B is about as exciting as watching paint dry and it will earn 8 percent annually. Account A will have the following returns over the five-year period: 20 percent, 21 percent, 10 percent, -17 percent, and 10 percent. Which would you choose? Let's see which one makes the best sense.

$100,000 Invested for Five Years		
	Option A	Option B
Year 1	+20%	+8%
Year 2	+21%	+8%
Year 3	+10%	+8%
Year 4	-17%	+8%
Year 5	+10%	+8%
Total	$?	$?

The answer is Option B.

$100,000 Invested for Five Years		
	Option A	Option B
Year 1	+20%	+8%
Year 2	+21%	+8%
Year 3	+10%	+8%
Year 4	-17%	+8%
Year 5	+10%	+8%
Total	$145,824	$146,932

It would have an ending balance of $146,932 versus Option A's ending balance of $145,824—and Option B had a little smoother ride along the way. Sure, Option A had some stellar years with huge rates of returns, but those four years of double-digit returns still could not make up for that one year in the red.

The Flaw of Averages (Or How to Go Broke Averaging 10+ Percent Annually)

One of Double M's favorite ploys is to use the Flaw of Averages. Here's how he did it with Lucky Larry.

When "Lucky" Larry was getting ready to retire, he visited the local fortune teller, who informed him the S&P 500 Index would average 10.6 percent for the next forty years. Since Lucky had socked away $1 million and had total confidence in the fortune teller's market prediction, he decided to withdraw $100,000 of income each year from his portfolio—after all, that's just a 10 percent withdrawal rate from a portfolio he believed would average 10.6 percent. How did Lucky's portfolio look forty years later? How much money did he have left?

The good news is Lucky did this in 1964, and the fortune teller was right! For the next forty years, the S&P 500 Index did indeed average 10.6 percent.

It sounds like Lucky got lucky, right?

Why, then, did he go broke in 1981, less than eighteen years after he started?

His $1 million was gone. He didn't get the benefit of the next twenty-two years of fantastic gains. What happened? Double M had fooled Lucky with the *Flaw of Averages*. Lucky had failed to recognize the difference between the market's actual *year-to-year performance* and its *average performance*. While the market did in fact average 10.6 percent for forty years, the market declines in the 1970s forced Lucky to take his income from a dwindling portfolio. When the market came back with good returns, he had less capital to benefit from the positive returns.

Lies, Damned Lies, and Statistics

Averages may be statistically true but still be lies. No family has 2.3 kids. The average temperature in Nashville may be 59.7 degrees, but the actual temperature is rarely 59.7 degrees. The stock market averages about 10 percent annually, but how often is the return actually 10–11 percent? How often has that happened out of the last ninety-eight years?

Once.

Just once.

From the end of 1925 through the end of 2023, the S&P 500 stock index averaged about 10 percent annually but produced a return between 10 and 11 percent in only one calendar year. In fact, the stock market rarely produces returns close to 10 percent in any given calendar year. To drive the point home, the stock market had a 20 percent or greater *loss* more times than it returned a *gain* of 8–12 percent. But that's only part of the story. The market's *gain* has been 20 percent or greater thirty-seven times out of those years. Losses of 20 percent or more have occurred in only six years.[11]

The stock market's returns don't go in a straight line. They never have. Expecting a return of 10–11 percent each year will leave an investor feeling off course almost every year.

The stock market is like electricity. If used prudently with solid risk-management tools and careful attention, electricity is a wonderful benefit, giving us lights, air-conditioning, and power to charge our phones. But when used carelessly, without proper respect and understanding, electricity can be ... well ... *shocking*. The market is the same way.

While it can bring tremendous gains, it can deal devastating losses for those who don't know what they're doing.

Cash Flow Matters

Referring to long-term averages can have some utility, particularly during the accumulation phase. It can serve as a lighthouse to encourage you to look past the current stormy waters and continue course. But during the income phase, the seas are less forgiving. Options for correcting errors are more constrained. If the boat gets swamped on the beach before leaving for the voyage, there is more hope of rescue. If the boat takes on water in the middle of the ocean, prospects for prosperity or survival are not as good.

Market Math loves to convince people to look at averages or historical returns without taking individual cash flow into account. Of course, no one knows what returns will be twenty years or twenty days into the future. But cash flow really does matter. The rules change depending on whether you're putting money in, taking money out, or doing neither one.

The following table shows the returns for two hypothetical investors who each invest $250,000.[12] Investor One gets the S&P 500 returns from the beginning of 1999 through the end of 2018. Investor Two gets the same returns *but in the opposite order* for this illustration.

We'll look first at the investors growing their money for twenty years (Growth Phase) and then, using the same scenarios, taking an income (Income Phase) from their portfolios for the next twenty years.

Growth Phase

Growth Phase: Two Portfolios.
Identical Returns in Reverse Order.

Annual Income Withdrawals: None
Starting Values: Investor One = **$250,000**   Investor Two = **$250,000**

	Investor One		Investor Two	
Year	Annual Return	Year-End Value	Annual Return	Year-End Value
1	21.04%	$ 302,604	-4.38%	$ 239,039
2	-9.10%	$ 275,054	21.83%	$ 291,225
3	-11.89%	$ 242,361	11.96%	$ 326,055
4	-22.10%	$ 188,798	1.38%	$ 330,567
5	28.68%	$ 242,954	13.69%	$ 375,817
6	10.88%	$ 269,392	32.39%	$ 497,537
7	4.91%	$ 282,625	16.00%	$ 577,161
8	15.79%	$ 327,263	2.11%	$ 589,349
9	5.49%	$ 345,243	15.06%	$ 678,125
10	-37.00%	$ 217,511	26.46%	$ 857,587
11	26.46%	$ 275,074	-37.00%	$ 540,299
12	15.06%	$ 316,509	5.49%	$ 569,982
13	2.11%	$ 323,193	15.79%	$ 660,007
14	16.00%	$ 374,915	4.91%	$ 692,426
15	32.39%	$ 496,343	10.88%	$ 767,777

Year	Investor One		Investor Two	
	Annual Return	Year-End Value	Annual Return	Year-End Value
16	13.69%	$ 564,285	28.68%	$ 988,010
17	1.38%	$ 572,094	-22.10%	$ 769,654
18	11.96%	$ 640,516	-11.89%	$ 678,175
19	21.83%	$ 780,351	-9.10%	$ 616,431
20	-4.38%	$ 746,137	21.04%	$ 746,137

	Investor One	Investor Two
Annual Internal Rate of Return	5.62%	5.62%
Value at the End of Year 20	$746,137	$746,137

Their results, predictably, are exactly the same.

Income Phase

When we get to the income phase, the rules change. We must realize that averages don't count; real results are what count. If history is any guide—and it's the only guide we have—we can look at the lessons of the past to make sure we aren't doomed to repeat its mistakes.

In the previous example, both investors had seen the value of a long-term perspective and approach. We can imagine both Investor One and Investor Two were fairly confident in their investment and in their ability to be good investors.

In this next example,[13] we'll start with the ending value Investor One and Investor Two got: $746,137. We will use the same investments and the same order of return in order to calculate their results for the next twenty years. They will both begin taking an income of 5.25 percent based on the $746,137 of capital. Each investor will increase their income by 3 percent annually to keep up with rising costs of living. Let's see how these disciplined investors fare over the next twenty-year period, getting the same results they got in the previous twenty years.

Income Phase: Two Portfolios.
Identical Returns in Reverse Order.

Annual Income Withdrawals:[14]   5.25 percent of first-year value
(increased 3 percent annually for cost of living)

Starting Values (First-Year Value): Investor One = **$746,137**
Investor Two = **$746,137**

Year	Investor One		Investor Two	
	Annual Return	Year-End Value	Annual Return	Year-End Value
1	21.04%	$ 859,540	-4.38%	$ 672,744
2	-9.10%	$ 743,499	21.83%	$ 775,427
3	-11.89%	$ 614,424	11.96%	$ 825,245
4	-22.10%	$ 439,780	1.38%	$ 793,582
5	28.68%	$ 514,440	13.69%	$ 855,815
6	10.88%	$ 521,451	32.39%	$ 1,080,990
7	4.91%	$ 498,451	16.00%	$ 1,202,426
8	15.79%	$ 524,589	2.11%	$ 1,178,322

Year	Investor One		Investor Two	
	Annual Return	Year-End Value	Annual Return	Year-End Value
9	5.49%	$ 503,625	15.06%	$ 1,305,578
10	-37.00%	$ 277,880	26.46%	$ 1,597,753
11	26.46%	$ 287,813	-37.00%	$ 960,954
12	15.06%	$ 270,083	5.49%	$ 956,924
13	2.11%	$ 220,255	15.79%	$ 1,049,207
14	16.00%	$ 195,621	4.91%	$ 1,043,084
15	32.39%	$ 191,749	10.88%	$ 1,096,154
16	13.69%	$ 152,620	28.68%	$ 1,344,214
17	1.38%	$ 91,437	-22.10%	$ 991,430
18	11.96%	$ 32,685	-11.89%	$ 814,413
19	21.83%	$ 0	-9.10%	$ 674,923
20	-4.38%	$ 0	21.04%	$ 743,272

	Investor One	Investor Two
Annual Internal Rate of Return	2.52%	6.81%
Value at the End of Year 20	$0	$746,137
Total Distribution	$ 952,060	$1,052,572

As these examples illustrate, something completely beyond a person's control (the sequence of returns) can have a tremendous impact on results. Portfolios that are merely diversified cannot protect an investor from declines. When markets begin to gyrate, many investments begin behaving alike. A dose of risk management allows investors to minimize the pain and potentially miss some of the downside. Diversification alone can't offer the same assurances.

Double M often lulls people into complacency. Just like these two investors had twenty years of seeing their money almost triple in value during their growth phase, that created tremendous confidence and even overconfidence. That can lead to complacency and an "if it ain't broke, don't fix it" mentality.

Double M smiles.

One Investment. Three Investors. Three Results.

Here is an example to show how one investment can have such dramatically different results depending on cash flow. Three investors invest in exactly the same investment whose share price is (for hypothetical purposes) updated once per year. One invests a $1 million lump sum and holds for growth (no cash flow). The second invests a $1 million lump sum and takes income from the money (cash flow out). The third investor invests $100,000 per year in ten installments for a total of $1 million invested (cash flow in). Each of the three owns exactly the same investment for the entire ten-year period.

Year	One-Time Lump Sum Investment of $1M	Lump Sum Investment Spending $50,000 Annually (5% of Initial Principal)	Dollar-Cost-Avg. with $100,000 for Ten Annual Installments	Investment Share Price
0	$1,000,000	$1,000,000	$100,000	$10
1	$800,000	$750,000	$180,000	$8
2	$600,000	$512,500	$235,000	$6
3	$500,000	$377,083	$295,833	$5
4	$400,000	$251,667	$336,667	$4
5	$300,000	$138,750	$352,500	$3
6	$400,000	$135,000	$570,000	$4
7	$500,000	$118,750	$812,500	$5
8	$700,000	$116,250	$1,237,500	$7
9	$900,000	$99,464	$1,591,071	$9
10	$1,000,000	$60,516	$1,767,857	$10
Final	$1,000,000	$60,516	$1,767,857	
Gain/Loss	$0	($439,484)	$767,857	

One investment with three dramatically different results.

The first investor broke even and made no money. The second investor lost his shirt. The third investor did okay, making more than 5.6 percent compounded annually, albeit with extreme drawdown in value.

All three investors show up at the same party. Investors One and Two scratch their heads trying to figure out why Investor Three is talking about how much money he made on this investment.

Double M smiles.

It takes all three superpowers to overcome Villain #6, Market Math—the dreaded Double M.

VILLAIN #7: YOUR BRAIN ON MONEY

We love dopamine. Dopamine is a neurotransmitter that plays a crucial role in our brain's reward system and motivates us to take action to achieve our goals. The anticipation of a reward triggers the release of dopamine in the brain's mesolimbic pathway, which includes the nucleus accumbens and the ventral tegmental area. These brain regions are involved in reward processing, motivation, and goal-directed behavior.

I'm by no means an expert on behavior or brain chemistry, but I have done some research on the brain's built-in reward system. As I understand it, you get a dopamine kick from anything that is associated with positive emotion. Our brains interpret that as an indication that we're moving toward a desired goal. That not only creates a sense of satisfaction but the dopamine also strengthens the circuits that are co-activated with those events, which provides a stronger internal drive to keep going, to keep progressing toward that goal.

Have you ever exercised stock options, sold something for a great profit, or seen an investment surge in price? If so, you probably felt this dopamine-driven reward cycle that made you feel good and pushed you to continue pursuing the goal in order to continue getting that "dopamine high." In this way, dopamine fuels our momentum, which plays a crucial role in helping us stay focused and motivated toward our goal. When we experience progress or success toward a goal, our brain releases more dopamine, which further reinforces our behavior and increases our drive to continue moving forward. This positive feedback loop associated with momentum helps us stay on track and increases our chances of achieving the goal. This is when that magnetic, compelling vision of the future comes into clear view.

While our brain's reward system is designed to motivate us toward goals, it may not be well-equipped to handle other modern challenges related to making good money decisions. The evolutionary purpose of dopamine was to drive our ancestors to seek basic rewards like food, shelter, and mates. In today's complex world, where financial decisions can have long-term consequences, our brain's reward system may lead us astray.

For example, the allure of quick financial gains through something like gambling may trigger a surge of dopamine that clouds our judgment and leads us to take unnecessary risks. The result can be impulsive decision-making and poor money management. Additionally, the constant stimulation of our reward system by modern technology, such as online shopping or gambling, can lead to addictive behavior and financial distress.

To overcome these challenges, it is important to be aware of how our brain's reward system influences our behavior. By understanding the neurological pathways involved in goal pursuit and the role of dopamine in motivation, we can better regulate our behavior and make informed choices. Setting clear goals, breaking them down into smaller tasks, and celebrating small victories along the way can help maintain momentum and increase our chances of success.

This is why many people elect to use a mathematical process when it comes to investments. Speaking from personal experience, I can certainly say that my decision-making is better when I use an algorithmic process instead of just going with my gut.

Basic Behavioral Finance Principles

There are some key concepts from behavioral finance everyone should be aware of. These concepts can affect us all, no matter how smart or disciplined we think we are. The bottom line is that you are in control of your own mind, and a better understanding of your mind can help you unleash your financial superpowers.

Loss aversion is a behavioral finance concept that suggests that we feel the pain of losses more acutely than the pleasure of gains. This bias can lead us to make irrational decisions when managing portfolios, as we may be more willing to take risks to avoid losses rather than to achieve gains. Understanding how loss aversion influences investor behavior is crucial for financial advisors and investors alike.

Research supports this idea that our brains tend to be more risk-averse when faced with potential losses compared to potential gains. According to prospect theory, developed by Daniel Kahneman and Amos Tversky, we experience losses approximately twice as strongly as gains of the same magnitude. This asymmetry in the way losses and gains are perceived can lead to suboptimal outcomes.

A study by Dr. Terrance Odean titled "Are Investors Reluctant to Realize Their Losses?" found that investors are often reluctant to sell losing investments due to the pain of realizing a loss. This phenomenon, known as the *disposition effect*, can lead to a reluctance to cut losses and move on to more promising investments.

One study conducted by Dr. Hersh Shefrin and Dr. Meir Statman, titled "The Disposition to Sell Winners Too Early and Ride Losers Too Long: Theory and Evidence," found that investors tend to hold on to losing investments for too long in the hope of recouping their losses, while they are quick to sell winning investments to lock in gains. This behavior can result in missed opportunities for portfolio growth and increased risk of incurring further losses.

SHORT-TERM TRADER ON THE UPSIDE

When I first started in financial services as a stockbroker, I met Buddy. He was a fine Southern gentleman with more country-isms than a character from *Hee-Haw*. I had bought into the concept adopted by most successful investors: Cut your losses short and let your profits run. He told me about something he owned, and I recommended he sell it. He declined and shared his logic.

"Son, you need to understand. I don't like to lose money. If I make money, I take my profit quick. If I buy something and it goes down, I wait until I get back to even. Even if it takes me years. I'm a short-term trader on the upside and a long-term investor on the downside."

I disagreed with this approach, but it was his money and ultimately his decision.

I didn't talk to Buddy again for several years. When we crossed paths again, he told me all about the incredible, profitable business he'd built. I was glad for him, but I was also curious about how his investing strategy had been working out for him.

As great as his business had been, Buddy had been much more successful at *preventing* his portfolio from being successful. He continued to sell his winners too soon and hang on to losers way too long.

He experienced the disposition effect.

While loss aversion is one of the biggest factors in behavioral finance, there are several others, including

- **Prospect Theory:** Prospect theory suggests investors tend to make decisions based on the potential outcomes rather than the probabilities or likelihood of those outcomes. This can lead to investors taking on more risk than they should in an attempt to recoup losses.

- **Herding Behavior:** Research has shown that investors tend to follow the actions of others, particularly during periods of extreme market volatility or losses. This can lead to investors panicking and selling their investments at a loss or, conversely, buying into a falling market in the hopes of recovering losses.

- **Regret Aversion:** Research has also shown that investors tend to avoid taking actions that may result in regret, such as selling an investment that subsequently recovers in value. This can lead to investors holding on to losing positions longer than they should, resulting in further losses.

- **Mental Accounting:** Investors tend to compartmentalize their investments into different categories (e.g., retirement savings, college fund), which can result in suboptimal decision-making when faced with losses in one category. For example, an investor may be more willing to take on additional risk in one category to make up for losses in another, leading to potentially risky decisions.

BLACKJACK

I can't talk about mental accounting without thinking of my friends Pete and Dee and a ski trip we all took several years ago.

When Pete and I left the hotel in Tahoe to go skiing one morning, his wife, Dee, parked herself at a blackjack table. When we returned from skiing late that afternoon, Dee was seated at the same blackjack table.

She saw us walking toward her table and said, "Pete, go to the ATM and get me some more money. I'm up three grand! You never leave the table when you're on a heater. Go, Pete." I sat down at the table next to Dee while Pete dutifully headed to the ATM, shaking his head slightly.

I said, "Dee, I don't understand. If you're up three grand, why do you need Pete to get you more money?"

She replied, "Because I was down five grand and now, I've made three of it back."

"So, you're down two thousand dollars?" I asked.

"If you want to look at it that way, I suppose. But I'm up three grand from the bottom."

That's mental accounting.

- **Gender Differences:** A study by Dr. Brad
  Barber and Dr. Terrance Odean titled "Boys
  Will Be Boys: Gender, Overconfidence, and
  Common Stock Investment" found that
  men are more prone to overconfidence and
  to taking excessive risks, leading to higher
  trading activity and lower returns. On the other
  hand, women tend to be more risk-averse and
  cautious in their investment decisions, leading
  to better performance over the long term.
- **Portfolio Monitoring Frequency:** Research
  has also shown that the frequency with which
  you look at your portfolio values can affect
  your decision-making. A study by Dr. Neil
  Stewart and colleagues titled "Investing for
  Retirement: The Moderating Effect of Portfolio
  Monitoring Frequency on the Relationship
  Between Risk and Returns" found that investors who check their portfolios frequently are
  more likely to make knee-jerk reactions to
  short-term market fluctuations. This can lead
  to increased trading costs, lower returns, and
  missed opportunities for long-term growth.

Past Performance Doesn't Mean Jack

There is no more misunderstood phrase in the investment lexicon than, "Past performance is no guarantee

of future results." You may have even found yourself saying, "I know past performance is no guarantee of future results, but how has this done?" We want to know. We're wired to know. And there's a reason.

Our minds are future-prediction machines. We want to know about the future. We want to eliminate uncertainty. Where there is an unknown or uncertainty, we make things up. We look at the past to get a sense of what the future might look like, and we do this in every aspect of our lives.

The risk is that we extrapolate to infinity and beyond. If the weather is getting colder and the days are getting shorter, we know that eventually spring will come around again. But when it comes to investments, if it's going up, it's easy to extrapolate that it will go up forever. If it's going down, it's easy to picture it going to $0 by 2:00 p.m. Usually, neither one is correct.

Our desire to avoid the pain of loss (and know the pleasure of dopamine) is a powerful bias built into our brains that can influence our behavior and lead to suboptimal decision-making. Understanding how these psychological factors affect your brain can help better guide you toward smart decisions about money and disciplined investment strategies. Recognizing the tendencies we have that can result in poor decisions, such as holding on to losing investments for too long, panic in the face of losses, loss aversion, herding behavior, and looking at our portfolios too frequently, can help us make better money decisions, avoid the pitfalls of irrational behavior, and unleash our superpowers.

Behavioral Finance

Behavioral finance has taught us that we experience losses with about two and a half times more intensity than a gain. Gains feel good but losses strike brutally at our emotional core. During times of stress, the human brain craves action. There is part of us that wants to scream, "Somebody do something!" when losses get bad enough. This is that voice that tries to entice us into the Dance of Disaster.

The Emotional Cycle of Investing

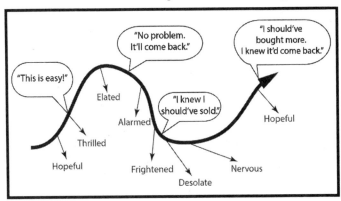

Many studies have pointed out the gap between stock market performance and performance of investors in stock funds. The gap points to decisions being made at moments of high stress. The emotion attached to losses can distort decision-making, causing a tendency to buy at the wrong time and sell at the wrong time. What feels right emotionally is to sell when things are down (because things are bad in the markets, the economy, and the world) and buy when prices are high (because the world looks rosy).

The emotional cycle of investing that goes along with a buy-and-hold (or buy-and-hope) approach has the heightened risk of emotional decisions when losses mount. It's easy to think you can stomach the risk until you're in the heat of the moment. That's why I like having a predetermined, probability-based, research-tested game plan. Should you know what conditions would constitute a sale or reallocation before you invest? Could an evidence-based exit point (instead of an emotional decision or a guru-based decision) be more effective?

In short, a game plan you're likely to stick with when markets are up or down has three ingredients:

1. How you'll behave in up markets
2. How you'll behave in down markets
3. How you'll distinguish between the two

Overcoming Your Brain on Money requires a healthy dose of the three fundamental financial superpowers.

CHAPTER 8

STRATEGIES TO DEFEAT YOUR VILLAINS

IN HIS BOOK *CHANGE OR DIE*, ALAN DEUTSCHMAN lays out three essential elements for change that genuinely lasts. The need for a lasting change resonated with me. Deutschman identifies the three elements or steps toward lasting change as

1. Relate—all lasting change starts with a relationship.
2. Reframe—all lasting change requires a reframing of thought and behavior.
3. Repeat—because we're all human, we have to repeat the same fundamentals to make change stick.

If you've completed the exercises along the way, you've had the chance to recall your own origin story, lay out your purpose, and complete your Wealth Roadmap. This is your Power of Purpose. Maybe you did this with your advisor. If so, that's a great way to develop (or deepen) a relationship. If you didn't do this with a trusted advisor, consider doing that—or finding a relationship that will work for you. Relate. Step one: check.

Hopefully, you now have (or have committed to get) a concrete, step-by-step plan of action. This is your Power of Plan. Your plan helps you reframe. Any action item you need to do, any behavior you need to change, or any sacrifice you need to make is now framed by how it impacts your goals. Change is reframed by its importance in achieving your goals that are important to you. Reframe. Step two: check.

Finally, the Power of Execution is all about repeating. We all fall off the wagon and go off plan sometimes. The critical question is, How do you crawl back on? Repetition is required. It's part of the human condition. Having a relationship and the reframing that comes with a plan can give us a helping hand back onto the wagon and a reminder of why. Repeat. Step three: check.

The three financial superpowers and the elements Deutschman lays out go hand in glove. Your Power of Purpose, Power of Plan, and Power of Execution have increased your financial strength. You understand how *your* focus on *your* plan for *your* reasons can overcome any of the Seven Deadly Financial Villains and some of the strategies they use.

While simply refocusing on your superpowers yields the power to vanquish the villains, it can be useful to have strategies or hacks to make it a little easier to accomplish.

ENLIST A SIDEKICK

Iron Man has Jarvis and Pepper Potts; James Bond has Q; Batman has Robin. Lewis Hamilton, the successful F1 driver, is the one behind the wheel and gets to hold the trophy, but the Mercedes-AMG Petronas team has more than a thousand professionals who design, develop, manufacture, and maintain the car and support Hamilton. Success rarely happens alone. Success is a team effort.

Who is (or should be) your sidekick? Who is on your team? You may want or need a sounding board, or an accountability partner. Or a coach. Or a full team of professional subject matter experts (tax, legal, asset management) helping you. I have used all of these, and you may want to also. The answers to who or what roles you need will be largely dependent on your personality and on the stage of life you find yourself. But having someone other than just you is helpful to most people. You don't have to go it alone.

BUILD A SHOCK ABSORBER

As a kid, we accept that superheroes fall out of the sky, land on one knee, bust the asphalt pavement into rubble, and do it with zero damage to their bodies. Any injuries they do acquire heal by the next scene or chapter. There are no concussions, torn Achilles tendons, blown-out ACLs or MCLs, and never a consideration for the g-forces endured. If only the real world were as forgiving.

An often-overlooked superpower is the ability to absorb shock and endure g-forces.

In the financial world, the equivalent of being slammed into the asphalt is the unexpected expense. Unexpected expenses come along with such regularity that we should ... *expect* them. Consistently, the biggest financial blunder we encounter is the lack of a financial shock absorber—which you may call your cash reserves, emergency fund, rainy day fund, line of credit, or slush fund.

People with first-generation wealth generally fall into one of two camps on financial shock absorbers (emergency funds):

1. They have virtually no liquidity (because they want *all* their money working for them)
2. They have more than they really need (because they never want to get caught without money they can easily get their hands on) and feel guilty about having that much money in liquid reserves

The key to getting the right amount—and having it guilt-free—is to have a well-thought-out plan with a rationale behind why that liquidity is there.

How much you really need depends on three factors:

- The consistency of your income
- The amount of your liquid assets compared to your regular expenses (income needs)
- Liabilities and potential liabilities

If you have a very consistent income (draw, salary, royalties, business income, etc.), three to six months of expenses plus any onetime expenses you're aware of in the next twelve months is in the right ballpark. For example, if you know you have to replace a car and your roof, then you'll want to have that amount plus a minimum of three months' worth of expenses tucked away.

If you have an income that fluctuates a great deal, you'll want to keep enough liquidity to cover six to twelve months of living expenses plus any onetime expenses you know will come up in the next twelve to eighteen months.

If your liquid or investment assets are more than ten times your regular income needs and known expenses, you may need only three to six months of expenses as a liquidity need. If your liquid investment assets are less than ten times your income needs, you probably need more.

Your liabilities and potential liabilities play a big factor also. If you have no debt and your home and all your vehicles are paid off, your liquidity needs are on the lower end of the scale. However, if you have family members that you may become financially responsible for, that can factor in as well.

The lack of a financial shock absorber is the most commonly occurring financial blunder we see the first-gen wealth make. Inevitably, a business opportunity or personal opportunity or the desire to help a family member comes along at the wrong time relative to investments. Having the shock absorber allows you to avoid cashing in investments that you want to leave on the tree until they're ripe.

AVOID THE MIKE TYSON PLAN

Mike Tyson, world heavyweight boxing champion and sometimes purveyor of financial advice, provides a good example. Like Pop said, you can learn something from everyone. It's well-documented that "Iron Mike" Tyson earned well over $400 million during his boxing career—and most of that money is gone. My point is not to throw punches at Mike Tyson; most of us have made money decisions we aren't particularly proud of (or maybe that's just me). The point is that it doesn't matter how much money you make when your spending outstrips it.

THE GOOSE AND THE GOLDEN EGGS

I love Margaret's story because it's a story of loss, grief, betrayal, being uprooted, being resilient, and coming out the other side enjoying life. It inspires me when I think of what she endured to get to where she is.

Margaret's husband, a cardiologist, died. It was a tragic situation. She was staying across the street from the hospital to be close to her ailing husband when she got the call he was fading. She crossed the street and, not wanting to wait for the elevator, she rushed up the stairs to get to his room. In the stairwell, she bumped into a physician, one of her husband's friends.

She ran into the room, but he was gone. He had just died minutes, maybe seconds, before she walked in.

In the aftermath of his passing, she discovered the physician she had bumped into in the stairwell had just left her husband's room. The dying doctor had asked his friend to sign as a witness to a last-minute revision to his will.

Margaret was horrified to discover what the changes were—and why her husband had made them.

In his final moments on earth, Margaret's husband changed his will to leave most of his estate…to his mistress. Unbeknownst to Margaret, he had been having a secret affair for years.

She fought the estate nightmare in court, of course, and she had won the case a short while before I met her.

She and her husband had traveled the world and accumulated a large wine collection, a farm, horses, and a fleet of cars. Like most first-gen wealth that we work with, Margaret didn't have a budget. She had never needed one. There was always ample income from her husband's cardiology practice to cover their extravagant lifestyle.

But now his income was gone. And even though the estate had been awarded to her, there was no new earned income to replace what she was spending and the upkeep on her lifestyle.

Once we have luxuries, we develop attachments and recategorize them as needs in our life. It's normal.

"Yes, we need both tractors and the skid steer."

"Yes, I need the Porsche, both Mercedes, the Lexus, and the pickup truck. Each vehicle has a specific purpose. How could I get along without all of them?"

"Yes, I need a house with seven bedrooms. Where else would my grandchildren stay the one week a year they visit?"

"And yes, the horses are expensive. Vets, farriers, fencing, feed. But they're so beautiful. And no, I can't ride them anymore. But I couldn't bear the thought of getting rid of a single one of them."

As we sat down to talk with Margaret about her situation, it became clear that, while she still had several million dollars of investments, land, and farm equipment, there were not enough assets to support the lifestyle she had enjoyed previously with her husband.

We sat at a round table in my office. I pulled out two pieces of yellow paper. I wrote "Annual Income for Life - $150,000" at the top of one page. On the other piece of paper, I wrote "The Mike Tyson Plan - $0."

I pushed both pieces of paper in front of her and said, "Here are two plans. One will pay you $150,000 per year to start, give you a raise every year, and last the rest of your life.

"The other one will give you a really fun four years of spending—like you're spending now—on whatever you want. But after four years, you will be broke, embarrassed, and homeless, and you'll probably need to move in with your children.

"Which one of these do you want to go with?"

She looked down at the two pieces of paper, sank in her chair, and pursed her lips.

"I do *not* want the Mike Tyson plan," she said flatly.

I picked up the Mike Tyson piece of paper, wadded it up, and threw it across the room.

She stared silently into my eyes.

"You have a goose," I said. "It will lay golden eggs for the rest of your life. The golden eggs are yours. Do what you want with them. But you've got to leave the goose alone. You can't cook the goose. You can't eat the goose. The goose is your principal. You have to take care of the goose, because it is literally going to feed you for the rest of your life. The goose can't take care of you if you start eating it."

I continued, "We can do this together. It will be hard. We will make it simple, but it's going to be incredibly hard. You've gone through an experience that I can't begin to imagine, and you've come out the other side. I know you have it in you. Beyond those beautifully manicured fingernails and your winning smile, I know there's a fighter in you who's going all the way to the bell. This is a new chapter of your life, and it's not what you had before—not even close. But you can still be happy."

It took more than a year to sell the farm, cars, and tractors and to build a house that better fit her new lifestyle. But she did it. Today, in fact, she's doing great.

Margaret was able to come back from her failing Mike Tyson plan, make the course corrections she needed to make, and most importantly, protect her golden goose.

STAY CASH CURRENT

When a payday happens years before you plan to live off your investments, staying cash current is an important concept. Exercising stock options and/or selling a business or significant asset can create a distracting situation: you're still working and earning an income, and you don't need that money *right then*— so you're stuck sitting there with a tempting pile of cash that seems to be begging you to blow it on something you don't need.

For example, let's say Fred leaves his C-suite job at age fifty, cashes in his company stock for fifteen times his annual income, and goes to work for a start-up. He enjoys working and plans to work for another ten to fifteen years because he feels like he wants to get "one or two more rodeos under his belt before he hangs up his spurs." So here is Fred who went from a C-suite job at $400,000 per year, cashed in $6 million of stock, and now works for a start-up making $175,000 per year.

When you have a payday that could fully fund your future retirement (Fred doesn't need the extra income now), it may require a shift in mindset. Thinking of that payday as prefunding your goals and creating a mindset of now working only to support your current lifestyle can be a helpful framework. No longer are you slogging away to set something aside for the future. The future is funded. All you have to do is knock out this month's expenses.

SECOND-GEN MARK

I had known Mark for years, and we had done things socially many times. He was a top-performing salesperson, but he never prioritized saving his income. His parents had been successful financially and had told Mark he didn't need to worry about money because they would certainly take care of him while still living and leave him plenty when they were gone. So, Mark spent everything he made and put his retirement hopes in his well-meaning parents' hands.

In his fifties, long after his father had passed away, Mark suggested that his mother invest in a project he and his partners were excited about and heavily committed to. Unfortunately, this was right before the Financial Crisis of 2008, which proved to be disastrous for the venture. Most of his future inheritance was lost.

His mother passed away a few years later. Despite the failed investment, she still left enough money for Mark to have a comfortable, mid-six-figure income for the rest of his life without having to save any of his working income.

The key for Mark was to stay "cash current." He simply needed to earn enough money to pay his bills and be careful to match his spending to his earnings. He had assets to support a substantial future income.

Staying cash current does two things. First, it establishes a baseline and builds the disciplines necessary to live within a certain financial framework. Second, it delays withdrawals from the portfolio so investments have more time to germinate and grow. Plus, delaying withdrawals means you'll depend on the investments for retirement for a shorter amount of time, thereby maximizing the funds in the portfolio.

I explained all this to Mark early enough to ensure he'd have plenty of money to maintain his high income well into retirement and for the rest of his life—as long as he stayed cash current.

He didn't.

Despite earning $300,000–500,000 per year from his successful sales job (and having done so for thirty years), Mark continued to pull money from his investments for two things: paying his taxes and paying off credit cards. This chipped away at his portfolio one chunk at a time for fifteen years. By the time he entered his seventies and his sales income began to decline, Mark was left with much less in his investments than he expected— too little to support the same kind of lifestyle he had always enjoyed.

He and his wife were forced to downsize, but they continued to travel the world and live a lifestyle their asset level couldn't support. They are in very real danger of outliving their investments and may ultimately find themselves completely broke in their eighties.

OUTSOURCE DISCIPLINE

Show me someone who is at the top of their game, whether they are a professional athlete, executive, physician, or songwriter, and I'll show you someone who has a coach, editor, collaborator, or someone who helps them stay on track. At some level, they outsource that discipline to someone else to help them execute.

It is always amazing to me how much more we accomplish when we are accountable to someone. If I'm paying a trainer and he tells me to do ten more push-ups, I do it. But if I'm by myself? Let's just say those extra ten become much less likely.

ACTION ON THE SIDE

In 2014 I came home and told my wife, Kelley, that we needed to talk. I had to make a confession.

"The good news is I haven't had an affair. The bad news is that I haven't been completely honest with you." Silence hung heavy in the air.

"Every month, for several years, before we send money from the business account to our personal account, I send money to a separate account that is in both of our names. Technically, you may have seen statements. They come to the house. But I know you don't usually look at them. Once a year, before tax time, I also disclose this income amount to the accountant to reconcile our books and make our taxes accurate. So, the bottom line is we have more money than you think we have."

Kelley stared expressionless at me a long moment before responding. "What you're telling me is that we have more money than I think we have. And we're still fine financially. Is that right?"

"Yep. That pretty much sums it up."

"You made it sound so serious. I thought it was something really bad. I thought you were going to tell me about someone named Sheila or Nancy. Well, if that's what you've been doing and it's working, I think you should just keep doing it and not tell me about it."

You can see from this story that I am clearly not here to give marital advice. And I'm not saying anyone else should do this. I am saying it is a tactic. And it worked for us and continues to be our method more than a decade later.

There is a key factor at work here: No one can outsource the discipline to execute unless they have a willingness to do so. We each must be coachable.

Early on in my career, I had a lot of resistance to coaching:

- "I can do this for myself."
- "I probably know more about this stuff than that guy does."
- "What can she teach me?"
- "It's too expensive."

It wasn't easy for me to get to the point of admitting to myself that I would probably be better off if I handed off a few responsibilities to someone better equipped to do them.

But I did, and I was.

CYNTHIA'S DISCIPLINE HACK

Cynthia is a Vanderbilt-educated attorney who came up in a time when women weren't attorneys. And if they were, they certainly weren't partners; they were closer to secretaries.

Regardless, Cynthia fought her way up the ladder and shattered glass ceilings. Along the way, she had children and later became a single mother and a respected professional. She learned by experience that if you have three kids, you'll have at least one difficult child. Many days, making it all work was a tough slog.

These days, she keeps a lot of irons in the fire—recently remarried, spending time with her grandchildren, hiking on four continents, and even opening her own specialty law firm.

Cynthia shared with me that discipline is always hard. "The goal is easy if all you have to do is set it," she mused. "It's actually doing the work to accomplish that goal that's really hard." So, Cynthia made the surprisingly difficult choice to outsource all the discipline to execute on her goals and inject a healthy dose of accountability into her workflow.

To make more progress on her health and fitness goals, she hired a personal trainer to come to her home several days a week and take her through an exercise regimen.

For her financial goals, she outsourced the discipline to our firm. During progress meetings, we lay everything out for her, give her the information she needs, list a few options, and tell her which option we prefer and why. Once she makes a decision on an issue, we advise her on what to do and then follow up to make sure she actually does it, making it as simple for her as possible.

Accountability is like tickling; you can't do it to yourself. If you truly want to make progress on your goals but struggle with the discipline to follow through, add a coach, advisor, mentor, or plain-old accountability partner to the mix. See how differently you attack your goals when someone's actually holding you accountable for them!

EMPLOY THE BOLDNESS OF ACTION

Goethe is attributed as saying, "Whatever you can do, or dream you can do, begin it. Boldness has genius, power, and magic in it!"

Action. Doing something, almost anything, can create energy.

This is true whether that action is selling your house, cleaning out the garage, moving, changing jobs, starting a relationship, ending a relationship, or starting a new training regimen. If you take bold action in one area, it becomes easier to take action in other areas of your life.

Too often, though, we get stuck in the complacency of "good enough." We get comfortable with how things are—good, great, or terrible—and we struggle with the motivation to make a change. Sometimes, having things going well is the worst thing for our goals, because we lose the motivation to dig in and put in the work required to make them better. We relax and do nothing, and as a result, our progress toward our goal gets stuck.

As author and business expert Jim Collins often says, good is the enemy of great.[15] When we take action on something significant, we are usually making a move away from good and toward great. Plus, action gets us unstuck. It gets us back in the game, back to working on something. The cool thing is, this action doesn't even have to be directly tied to the goal you want to impact. The simple act of making progress in one area puts us in a more active mindset that in turn ignites a renewed motivation to progress in all areas.

Stasis yields stasis, but movement builds momentum. If you need to make a change, I found it's easier to change when there is already change going on in your life.

USE THE SPILLOVER EFFECT

Boldness of action can lead to the Spillover Effect—tying two things together. That is, success in one area of life can translate success into another area of life.

The success you feel from staying with a new training program, despite the soreness, can "spill over." Tackling that thing at work—the position you need to hire or fire—can spill over. Doing the discipline you need to do for self-care—maybe making time for prayer, meditation, morning walks, or Pilates—can create that Spillover Effect. Using your dopamine-induced momentum in one area of life can spill over in a positive way to other aspects of your life.

ESTABLISH FEEDBACK LOOPS

Feedback loops are incredibly effective because they gamify our behavior.

In 2003, Garden Grove, California, confronted a problem that afflicts most of America—drivers speeding through school zones.[16] Authorities tried many tactics, including bright speed limit signs and policemen ticketing speeding motorists during drop-off and pickup times, with limited success. Speeding cars continued to hit bicyclists and pedestrians.

City engineers decided to take a different approach. They put up dynamic speed displays, or driver feedback signs—a speed limit posting, coupled with a radar sensor with an LED display showing the driver's speed.

The signs didn't tell drivers anything they didn't already know, as every car already has a speedometer. There were also no negative consequences, as no tickets were issued during this experiment. The results were fascinating nonetheless. Drivers slowed down an average of 14 percent. In fact, in many of the school zones, drivers' average speeds dropped to *below* the posted speed limit.

The signs leveraged a feedback loop, which research has shown is profoundly effective for changing behavior. Feedback loops involve four distinct stages. First comes the data. It must be measured, captured, and stored. Second is the relevance stage. The data must be displayed in a way that makes it emotionally relevant and compelling. The third stage is the consequence. The information must allow us to figure out alternate paths ahead. Finally, the fourth stage is action.

This framework has been shaped and refined by researchers for ages. Eighteenth-century engineers developed regulators and governors to control steam engines and other mechanical systems, which was an early application of feedback loops that later became codified into control theory.

The potential of the feedback loop to affect and alter behavior was explored in the 1960s by Albert Bandura, a Stanford University psychologist. He observed that giving individuals clear goals and a means to evaluate their progress toward that goal greatly increased the likelihood that they would achieve it. He later expanded that notion into self-efficacy, which holds that the more we believe we can meet a goal, the more likely we will do so.

Angry Birds, the smartphone game, is an example of a feedback loop. We take action (i.e., fire a bird from a slingshot) and are shown dotted lines indicating its projected flight path as well as the flight path of the previous bird, giving us contextually relevant information we can use to adjust the next bird's aim. This feedback loop—the dotted trajectory—which many video games do not give, may explain the popularity and satisfaction many people felt playing the game.

The link between action and consequence often gets lost when it comes to our money. What if you had a clear target? What if your behavior was creating a clear trajectory and it was easy to get visual feedback on how close you are to—or how far away you are from—your goal? What if you could track money decisions like you track your steps on an Apple Watch or how a continuous glucose monitor (CGM) tracks your blood glucose? If we had this kind of feedback on our money, we could make better decisions. The thing is, through technology, you can get that kind of feedback. Feedback loops allow us to correct our behavior and prevent accidents—automobile or financial—before they happen.

The real power of feedback loops is in giving people more control over themselves. Having better control of your money ensures that you control your money and that your money doesn't control you.

MAKE IT PERSONAL

An account titled "Individual account AJ-457293-01" may be a perfectly valid account title. But an account titled "Annual European Vacation AJ-457293-01" may have more emotional energy attached to it. Research has repeatedly shown that accounts with specific, personally meaningful titles are very motivating to investors.

Consider renaming your accounts so that each account has a title that reminds you what job those dollars have and what they need to accomplish.

ELIMINATE A NEGATIVE

Because the brain's wiring causes us to hate losses twice as much as we love gains, it may be easier to set up your environment to eliminate a negative rather than to create a positive.

You may have the money to put an 80 percent down payment on a house, but know that no matter what you put down, you will obsess about paying off the mortgage years early in a way you wouldn't obsess about accumulating a nest egg. Therefore, behaviorally, it may make sense to invest some of the money. You might put 40 percent in investments for wealth building and only put a 40 percent down payment on your home. Then, you could get laser-focused on eliminating the mortgage, knowing you wouldn't have nearly the same amount of emotional energy and motivation to save money for investing as you would to attack that mortgage debt.

ALAN'S 'VETTE

Alan was a hardworking man with a high school diploma and a PhD from the School of Hard Knocks who had a slight obsession with racing cars. He explained to me how he allowed himself to become obsessed with a particular car until he finally broke down and borrowed money to buy it. As soon as he did, though, he became just as obsessed with paying the car loan off as quickly as possible. He explored ways to grow his business, he beat the bushes to get more work for his crews, and he paid the loan off much faster than even his own ambitious plans predicted. Then, once the pressure and excitement died down, he bought another car and repeated the entire process.

Alan did this at least three times that I know of. It seemed crazy to me (and still does), but I at least understand his deep need to pay off those car loans. He was *driven* (pardon the pun) to eliminate the negative—in this case, his car loans. That motivation enabled him to grow his business and income to record heights in record time. As soon as the car loans were paid, though, he backed off and his productivity returned to normal levels. This showed me that he certainly *could* generate significant cash flow quickly for investing purposes *if he wanted to.* The problem was that he simply couldn't drum up the same passion for investing that he could for paying off debt.

A word of warning here. Don't get too leveraged or too deep in debt to motivate yourself. It is easy to slip to the dark side with this strategy, so you'll want to discuss this plan with at least two or more trusted sources before doing it. Creating a negative just to get motivated to eliminate it can be an extremely high-risk strategy. Leverage is a two-edged sword with very sharp blades. If you ever employ this strategy, you'll want to keep the size of the "negative" small enough that if something goes wrong, you'll still be able to manage the financial consequences without a lot of heartburn.

AUTOMATE

Automation is all about setting up your environment for success. Thousands of Americans participate in auto-enrollment in their 401(k), meaning that, if they don't opt out, they are automatically enrolled in the retirement plan to defer a portion of their income each pay period.

You can do the same thing for yourself. Set a monthly amount to automatically go into an investment account, whether it is $25,000 per month or $250 per month. The discipline of investing every month (even if you don't really see it and it is done automatically) is a great discipline to develop. It creates a habit of investing and of living on less than you earn.

Where are areas of your financial life you can automate for your success?

INSTALL THE ONE-WAY DOOR

I was very fortunate to find a partner who looks at money invested the same way I do. Once money goes into an investment account, it stays there. It doesn't come out because we want new furniture or a new car or anything else. It stays. The door only swings one way.

Now, of course, there will come a time that a consistent amount of income comes out of the account each month for living expenses. But that day is not today or tomorrow. Taking money out of the account for any reason would feel like a violation, like stealing it from its intended purpose.

This one-way-door mentality (which applies to both retirement and nonretirement accounts) is very different from the emergency / rainy day / slush fund account we have as a shock absorber against life's unexpected expenses.

The one-way-door agreement is a mentality we see across the spectrum with successful first-gen wealth clients.

TURN ON YOUR X-RAY VISION

Other than flying, X-ray vision is one of the most wished-for superpowers. Fortunately, you can access your own version of X-ray vision.

All it takes is to reconnect with the first fundamental superpower. Going back to your deep why, tapping into your moral code, and reviewing your Wealth Roadmap can help you see through the fog of whatever is right in front of you to the core of why.

Reviewing your Wealth Roadmap at least a couple of times a year may be a good use of sixty seconds of your time. It is for me.

K-CAR DREAMING

I started full-time in financial services as a stockbroker at a regional brokerage firm in Nashville, Tennessee, in the early 1990s. Once I passed a couple of securities exams, was licensed, and ready to go live, the branch manager gave me my sixty-second sales training.

"I guess you have a list of people to call. If you don't, there's a phone book in your desk. There's a clipboard up front with our tax-free municipal bond inventory on it. I suggest you pick one of those from the inventory and cold-call people. Make sure you don't ask them to buy less than $50,000 worth of bonds. There's a computer on your desk. If you don't know how to use it, ask somebody sitting around you. I don't know anything about computers." Then he turned and walked away.

At that moment, my sales training had ended, and I was terrified. I had seen the movie *Wall Street*, but that was the extent of my nonacademic financial education. I didn't know anyone that I thought would even have $50,000 to their name.

A whole new career as a stockbroker had sounded like a great idea at the time. I had quit my job writing at a public relations firm to work on several residential properties I purchased to flip. I had trouble moving them as fast as the infomercial said I would if I bought their course. After months of eighteen-hour days, I had finally dug myself out of a deep financial hole and was ready for a fresh start.

But now, here I was, out of the frying pan and into the fire.

After one day of randomly cold-calling my way through the phone book, I got in my car and drove to neighborhoods with big houses, wrote down the names of the streets, and went to the public library to use the reverse directory to get a better list.

A few days later, I discovered treasure in my desk. Like a scene from the movie *Glengarry Glen Ross*, I found the magic list of leads, hidden away at the back of a drawer.

The pot of gold I had found was a stack of three-by-five cards with the names of a business, its owner, phone number, notes, and the date of the last phone call, which all seemed to be about two years prior.

The notes on virtually every card read: "No money now. He's reinvesting everything back into the company. No liquidity. Check back in six months."

Pay dirt.

Over the next several days, I enthusiastically called every lead in that stack of note cards. On the other end of the phone line, I heard every one of them say the same thing. "I don't have any money now. I'm reinvesting everything back into my business. Check back with me in six months."

I was shocked. How could this be? Two years prior all these people felt certain that in six months they would have money, cash flow, liquidity to invest. And yet, two years later, no one appeared to be in a liquid position. So, either they had all gotten together and agreed on the same script to get rid of cold callers, or most of them suffered from the same affliction. Or a combination of the two.

I began looking for business from a number of different sources. But for the next three years, I would check back with those business owners every six to nine months. I learned to ask better questions. I discovered most of the small business owners didn't have retirement accounts, weren't investing on a systematic basis, and most were not investing outside of retirement accounts on a regular basis.

I learned two things from that experience. One is that there is no free lunch, magic bullet, or real shortcut around doing the work.

Second, to the best of my ability, I wanted to make sure I did not fall into the trap of having my personal life fund my business—I wanted there to be enough free cash flow to have some modicum of freedom. So, I made it a policy in my life to look at my business and my career as something to fund my life. I didn't want my career to completely control my life; I wanted my life to control my career. Therefore, I was able to take the advice of the late, great sales coach Jim Rohn and live on a fraction of what I earned. I began investing every month.

Everything has consequences.

Living on a fraction of what I earned meant people at work poked fun at me for not joining a country club and chided me for buying dress shoes from Shoe Carnival. Guys would shake their heads and chuckle as I pulled into my parking spot to park my $1,500 pickup (before I had the money to upgrade to a $2,300 Chrysler K car) between a Lexus and a Mercedes.

Fast-forward thirty years, and not one of those business owners from those lead cards ever become a client. No one who poked fun at me from those early years is living on their own private island, and most are still working to pay for something. And things worked out fine for us.

THE POINT OF NO RETURN

At times when several of the Seven Deadly Financial Villains show up all at once, we need a different way to think of things—to reframe them—so that we stay on plan and continue to execute.

Myra was a widow who was referred to me by her CPA. Her husband, Marty, had been a symphony and orchestral musician. Together, they had traveled the world. Now in her seventies, she dealt with depression and mental health issues.

She would sometimes call with anxiety about her money. I discovered a strategy that helped her put things in perspective when something she saw on TV or read in a newspaper caused her anxiety to flare up.

I used some quick math to calculate how long her money would last if she continued spending the way she'd been spending and earned 0 percent return on her money for the rest of her life.

That simple exercise routinely revealed that her money would last to support her to around age one hundred and thirty-seven. That usually quelled her anxiety—at least for another week or two, when another headline would freak her out and get her calling us again.

This same "zero return" exercise might work for you too. If you find yourself occasionally getting anxious about whether you have enough money saved in your investments, run the numbers to see how long your portfolio will support your lifestyle under this worst-case scenario. Assuming you have some significant savings, you may be surprised at how long your runway is before you'd have a real cash flow problem.

You have a plan you need to consistently execute. At this point, you know you have (or will soon get) a plan for up markets, a plan for down markets, and a clear way to know the difference. There isn't a scenario where you're unprepared. Realizing that you need to stay on plan is your best plan of action. The "no return" strategy may help you get or stay there.

DISTINGUISH WANT VS. NEED

If you wrestle with the Lever Denier or experience anxiety around trying to figure out how to adjust the spending lever, you may appreciate this strategy.

Try listing all your expenses on one spreadsheet or sheet of paper and then categorizing whether it's a need or a want. For example, you could list health insurance as a need. You could list your health club

membership as a want. You could list car insurance as a need. You could list a $1,500-a-month car
payment or lease payment as a want. Or you could list
25 percent as a need and 75 percent of the payment
as a want.

Categorizing each expense as a want or a need
brings clarity. It shows you all the things you *are*
spending money on that you don't *have* to spend
money on. This is especially helpful when we're
looking for ways to trim our monthly expenses and/or
ways to "find" money to invest.

As you go through this exercise, it may help to
enlist your sidekick to check your work. We all tend
to categorize some wants as needs, so be sure to inject
a little objectivity—and honesty—to this exercise by
getting someone else's opinion.

ADD ONE MORE ZERO

Zero is a fascinating concept; it's a number that
represents *nothing*. Depending on whose research you
believe, it was "discovered" either by the Babylonians,
Indians, Chinese, or the Sumerians and spread across
the Arab and African worlds before being introduced
to the West by Fibonacci, the Italian mathematician.

Regardless of who originally articulated the
concept, imagine what would be different in your life
if you woke up this morning and your portfolio and
your net worth had one more zero at the end? Or two

more zeros. What if your net worth changed overnight from, say, $2 million to $20 million? Or from $10 million to $100 million?

Jim Rohn once said, "The major question to ask on the job is not 'What are you *getting*?' The major question to ask on the job is 'What are you *becoming*?'"[17] At some level, making smart decisions about your money is very similar because it's not just about what we're getting; it's about who we are becoming.

Consider: How would one more zero make you think about your time? Would it bring more focus? What would you start doing? What would you stop doing? Would you focus less on details or more? Is there something you'd do differently with your time? Would you be engaged in all the same activities then that you are now?

How would one more zero make you think about your purpose? Is there something you'd bring into your life, or are there things you'd take out of your life? Would anything shift for you?

How would one more zero make you think about the process for making money decisions? Would you keep doing what you're doing, or would you hire a team of world-class experts to help you? Would you implement a process with accountability, clear benchmarks, a 107-point checklist to work through every year to make sure your financial house gets in order and stays in order? Would you use a precise system of checks and balances? Would you set up feedback loops to simplify the complex?

How would one more zero prompt you to communicate differently with your family about how to steward money? Research has consistently shown that about 90 percent of the time, family wealth is gone by the third generation. The interesting thing is that the 10 percent that continue to preserve wealth generation after generation have some things in common. Would it become important to learn what those common characteristics are and how to put them into practice in your family? (If so, there are many good books and coaching programs focused on multigenerational wealth transfer principles.)

How would one more zero make you think about your health? No one I know would say that money is more important than health. And yet you probably know people who live like it is. They know where the Dow closed but don't know their blood pressure. They know the P/E ratio of the S&P but don't know their cholesterol numbers. They know when their next report is due for work but don't know when they'll exercise again. Would one zero change anything for your health?

How would one more zero make you think about your personal relationships? Would it remove tension, add tension, or change the focus? How would the dynamics change? Rarely does an extra zero or two show up overnight. But if it did, what would you do? The more important question may be: What if you lived as though that extra zero was already there? What would be the impact?

You've accomplished a lot and covered a lot of financial real estate in this book. We've explored why first-gen wealth has navigation challenges with one foot in the life you came from and one foot where you are today. You've had the opportunity to think about your own situation, your origin story, your purpose, your plan, and how you execute. We've explored the inescapable realities of your money galaxy and identified the Seven Deadly Financial Villains determined to deter you.

And, in the back of your mind, you've had time to think about what's next for you.

What happens when you finish this book? Will anything be different for you? What will you do differently? Do you have a game plan for what you want to get done? Will this be just another book you've read, or will this play some part—a turning point—in your story? Will you do what you need to do to close that gap between where you are and who you are now and where you have the potential to go and who you want to be? Are you willing to be intentional so you have the highest probability to live the life you want to live and do what you want to do?

Maybe you've created a checklist (or decided to use the action checklist for this book). Maybe there are some things that need to be shored up for you. That may include completing or updating your Wealth Roadmap, clarifying your Power of Purpose, or connecting with your financial origin story. Maybe you have thought about updating or evaluating your plan—or even getting a real game plan for the first time. Maybe you've made a mental list of how you're going to execute or implement differently. Whatever that is for you, I want to encourage you to do it. There is boldness in action.

There's good news and there's bad news. The good news is that it's up to you to make it happen, just like it's been all along. The bad news is that it's up to you to make it happen, just like it's been all along.

The stakes have never been higher for you than they are today. What's at stake is the life you want. You know this. The Evil Clock knows this.

There's one more thing you may want to know before we finish up.

It's the big payoff.

The ultimate asset.

CHAPTER 9

THE ULTIMATE ASSET

Y OU'VE BEEN IN THIS EPIC BATTLE TO FORGE AND fortify your financial superpowers to yield the life you want, to do what's important to you, and to live out your mission and values. You've encountered numerous pitfalls, setbacks, and villains along the way. With your destination in sight, a question (or two) often arises.

Is there more?

Is there something missing?

Like Pop said, money doesn't buy happiness, but neither does poverty!

What is this ultimate asset? Is it a new form of cryptocurrency, non-fungible tokens, private equity, rare earth metals, rare art, artificial intelligence, or something completely different?

The best way to understand the ultimate asset is with two short stories.

Recently I spoke with a successful entrepreneur who asked about creating a Wealth Roadmap for himself and his wife. But he didn't want to take the time for the most skippable of the superpowers—the Power of Purpose. He was in a hurry to get to the bottom line, to talk about making more and more money. That was his ultimate focus. He wanted to know about our quantitative investment approach because he wants a private jet. I asked him, "What then?" He said when he buys one private jet, his next step is to get two. "You can never have enough!" he said. That's where every question led: You can never have enough.

I felt uneasy, so after a short conversation, I wished him well in all he endeavors in life and excused myself.

From my experience with the people I've worked with, I've found that it's easy to create your own hamster wheel, to try to use money to scratch an itch that money can't reach. Winning the rat race is a great accomplishment if your ultimate purpose is to be the fastest rat. Everyone gets to make choices.

Years ago, when I first completed my Wealth Roadmap, I had no inkling what the unintended and unexpected consequence would be. That roadmap would lead me to the ultimate asset.

The second story to explain the ultimate asset is through a story about two men, both famous authors. Kurt Vonnegut, author of *Slaughterhouse-Five*, originally told the story through a poem he penned to honor his deceased friend, Joseph Heller. Heller authored *Catch-22*, which was turned into a movie. The *New Yorker* published Vonnegut's poem in May 2005. Here's my paraphrase of the poem (and my favorite money story):

Vonnegut and Heller were at a party thrown by a billionaire hedge-fund manager at Shelter Island, Long Island, New York. It's in the high-rent district on Long Island.

Vonnegut turned to Heller and asked him how it made him feel to know that their host may have made more money in one single day than Heller had made in his entire career from *Catch-22*.

Heller turned to Vonnegut and said, "I have something that he can never have."

Looking around at the lavish estate, Vonnegut must've been perplexed before he asked, "What on earth could that be, Joe?"

We can only imagine that Heller allowed a pregnant pause before answering, "Enough."

Enough. The ultimate asset. The ultimate superpower.

What I had the privilege to learn from people who have the ultimate asset of enough is this:

- Money serves them; they don't serve money.

- Money is a means, not an end.
- Their mission, vision, and purpose are clear.
- Their Power of Purpose provides absolute clarity about what's important and why.

The resulting outcome—the pattern—is that they overwhelmingly have a sense of contentment, gratitude, generosity, and graciousness.

My hope is that you unleash your financial superpowers and optimize your potential so you have that ultimate asset—enough—and everything that comes with it.

ACKNOWLEDGMENTS

I'D LIKE TO ACKNOWLEDGE THE FOLLOWING PEOPLE, without whom this work would not have been possible:

First, my wife Kelley who gave me encouragement, space, and always supports our next "adventure."

The entire team at Luken Wealth Management for continuing to raise the standard.

The team at Forefront and editor Allen Harris. It's great to work with professionals who care about quality. I appreciate the willingness to challenge me so that we could deliver the best work possible.

Lastly, much gratitude to the clients I've had the privilege to work with for years (and decades). You've taught me so much—without you, this book wouldn't have existed! I'm reminded of the words of Jim Rohn, who said that most people ask, "What will I get out of a job?" But the important question to ask is: "Who will I become?" Who I have become is a direct reflection of your influence and the impact of our relationship. It's an honor to continue to serve you.

NOTES

1   "Charles Schwab Modern Wealth Survey 2023," Charles Schwab
    & Co., accessed March 25, 2024, https://content.schwab.com/
    web/retail/public/about-schwab/schwab_modern_wealth_
    survey_2023_findings.pdf.

2   "Survey of Consumer Finances (SCF)," Federal Reserve Board,
    updated 2022, https://www.federalreserve.gov/econres/scfindex.
    htm.

3   Thomas Piketty and Emmanuel Saez, "The Evolution of Top
    Incomes: A Historical and International Perspective," Working
    Paper No. 11955 (National Bereau of Econmic Research, January
    2006), https://www.nber.org/papers/w11955.

4   "Five Habits of 401(k) Millionaires," Fidelity, https://www.fidelity.
    com/viewpoints/tcm:526-124671-9451.comp?source=content_
    type%3Areact%7Cfirst_level_url%3Aarticle%7Csection%3Amain_
    content%7Cbutton%3Abody_link.

5   *World Ultra Wealth Report 2021 Findings* (Wealth-X, 2021), https://
    go.wealthx.com/world-ultra-wealth-report-2021.

6   Joe Maciariello, "Joe's Journal: On Creating the Future," The
    Drucker Institute, published May 24, 2011, https://drucker.
    institute/thedx/joes-journal-on-creating-the-future/.

7   Robert B. Cialdini et al. "The Role of the 'Because' Condition in
    Compliance with a Request," *Journal of Personality and Social
    Psychology* 36, no. 4 (1978): 414-22.

8   Cialdini, "Role of the 'Because' Condition."

9   Tom Peters, "Brand You: You Are Your Calendar," posted July 23, 2010, by Tom Peters, YouTube, 2 min., 27 sec., https://www.youtube.com/watch?v=3cgn7qtwMh8.

10   Jim Rohn, "3 Money Habits That Separate the Rich from the Poor," Jim Rohn International, February 15, 2017, https://www.jimrohn.com/3-money-habits-separate-rich-poor/.

11   The S&P 90 was introduced in 1928 and later expanded into the S&P 500. Prior to this, other data sources, such as the Cowles Commissions, were used. Robert Shiller, the author of *Irrational Exuberance*, compiled the data sources that extend back to 1871, and DQYJD further streamlined that data. You cannot invest directly in an index.

12   Luken Investment Analytics, Morningstar Direct, August 2019.

13   Luken Investment Analytics, Morningstar Direct, August 2019.

14   Withdrawals are taken at the end of each month after monthly investment growth. For example, 5.25% of $746,137 = $39,172.22. For year one, $39,172.22 ÷ 12 = $3,264.35 per month. In all subsequent years, they are adjusted up by 3.00% at year end. For year two, $3,264.35 x 3.00% + $3,264.35 = $3,362.28 per month.

15   Jim Collins, *Good to Great* (HarperCollins, 2001), 1.

16   Thomas Goetz, "Harnessing the Power of Feedback Loops," *Wired*, June 19, 2011, https://www.wired.com/2011/06/ff-feedbackloop/.

17   Jim Rohn, *The Art of Exceptional Living* on cassette tape.